Stranger in the Mirror

Erin LeBlanc

The Search for Me

STRANGER IN THE MIRROR

THE SEARCH FOR ME

ERIN LEBLANC, MEd, LLM
SPEAKER | LGBTQ ADVOCATE | AUTHOR

 Daring to Share Global

Published by Erin L. LeBlanc,
June 2020 - 9781777273804

Editor: Diana Reyers
Typeset: Greg Salisbury
Book Art and Cover Design: Ollie Greenwood-Vidal

My two amazing daughters,
you are a never-ending source of joy and strength.

Julie, my life partner, is my anchor and my soft place to land.

I am forever grateful for their ongoing love and support.

Praise for the Book

A human life, fully lived, is at its core a journey of healing and transformation. Because she well knows how painful and lonely that journey can be – the path she travelled was rockier than most – Erin LeBlanc shares her unique story with unflinching honesty in the hope that: "this memoir provides some degree of solace."

Stranger in the Mirror is both an illuminating crash course on Gender Dysphoria, and a powerful personal account of prevailing over doubt and suffering to surface, through courage and self-knowledge, into confidence and empowerment.

Erin's story shows that neither genetics nor upbringing are life sentences, and that even with seven arrows through the heart, healing is always possible. It did bring me solace, and even a good measure of these most fleeting of feelings – hope and gratitude.

Benoit-Antoine Bacon, President and Vice-Chancellor
Carleton University, Ottawa, Ontario, Canada

Praise for the Book

A poignant, deeply insightful, and courageous memoir of the journey to self-acceptance. Through journal excerpts, and heart breaking anecdotes, Erin shares her vulnerability, her challenges, and, ultimately, her resilience. The reader is compelled to reflect on the impact and role of gender—and often assumed gender—in our relationships with others and with oneself. Erin's bravely candid and moving struggle to understand and accept her true identity should be required reading for anyone experiencing gender dysphoria or seeking to be a better ally.

Stacy G. Kelly, Director, Philanthropy,
The 519 Church Street Community Centre,
Toronto, Ontario, Canada

Erin's story is one of resilience and determination, of overcoming tremendous obstacles on her journey to becoming her authentic self. Her work as an advocate for the transgender community, particularly in respect of health care and access to legal and health services, is helping to ensure that others do not experience the same struggles. For her work in establishing transgender transitioning guidelines and identifying and removing barriers for individuals transitioning in the workplace, Erin was named a recipient of the Queen's University Tri-Award for the promotion of accessibility, equity, and human rights. A truly motivational speaker, her contributions are helping to make positive changes in our communities. Stranger in the Mirror is a great read for anyone in the LTGBTQ+ community, their families and allies, and those looking to better understand the strength required to be your authentic self.

Teri Shearer, Deputy Provost, Academics and Inclusion
Queen's University, Kingston, Ontario, Canada

Praise for the Book

It's been a tremendous pleasure getting to know Erin over the last few years. She is incredibly active and engaged, a strong advocate for our LGBTQ community, and she is an amazing supporter of young people in Kingston.

Bryan Paterson, Mayor, City of Kingston, Ontario, Canada

A heroic tale of following one's path with guts, courage and awareness. I learned so much from this beautifully written story of Erin's transition to 'what needed to be'.

Dr. Peter Jensen, Founder, Third Factor Inc.,
Toronto, Ontario, Canada

When a transgender person goes through their struggles, and later their coming out and transition, it is a unique path which becomes more manageable when you are able to share it with others who understand what you are going through. I was fortunate to become friends with Erin while we were both working through our feelings which allowed us to support each other as part a group of friends all on similar paths in life. Even though we had miles between us, we all were connected in ways that bonded us forever. Erin's story takes you through her experiences and feelings that allow insight into her struggles and emotions just as I saw them happening. Her story is one that is uniquely Erin's and engaging in its portrayal.

Sue Robbins, Transgender Advisory Council, Equality Utah
Past Board Chair, Utah Pride Center, Utah, United States

Praise for the Book

To be immersed in Erin's story was an experience unlike any I ever had as a witness to authenticity. Her struggle as a transgendered woman and journey to living her authentic self, took me to heartbreaking places. Her words captured her emotional process and inner life in a way that was completely inescapable. I mourned with her in her suffering and cheered her in her transformation. As a gay man, I celebrate her incredibly courageous story, and know how important it is that we carry on the legacy of these stories from members of our tribe. Erin shares a powerful message – our need for society's evolution in a new reality and language for gender identity that includes embracing everyone with unconditional acceptance. We must all live without fear of being our authentic selves. Otherwise we will perpetuate tremendous suffering. I have no doubt Erin will continue to inspire and lead us as a true hero in the cause for authenticity, compassion, and social evolution.

John De Freitas, Authentic Leadership Coach,
Published Co-Author, Daring to Share: There to Here,
2nd Edition | Volume 1, Vancouver Island, Canada

Beautifully written, raw, and honest. Erin writes with such courage to show all her truths behind her life's journey. This book will help transgender people and actually anyone struggling to find out who they really are on the inside. Honoured to have the opportunity to read this story. Thank you for your bravery. Welcome Erin.

Maureen Rooney, RN Paediatric and Trauma Nurse
Toronto, Ontario, Canada

Praise for the Book

My long-time colleague and friend, Erin Leeann LeBlanc, has written a moving and thoughtful account of the journey to her true self. Her courage and generosity of spirit are inspiring. No matter what our path in life, we can all learn from the lived experience of the transgender community. Empathy is the bond that holds society together and I have no doubt that Erin's story will inspire a broader understanding of the transgender community, helping to build those bonds of empathy that are never more important than today.

Bill Flanagan, President and Vice-Chancellor,
University of Alberta, Canada

In Stranger in the Mirror, Erin shares a raw, poignant and honest account of self-discovery that can help people to understand what it's really like to go through gender transition. It is impossible for a cisgender person to truly understand the lived experience of a person going through such a journey, but in sharing her story, Erin is helping bring people a little closer to that understanding by building empathy for others.

Michael Bach, CCDP/AP,
Chief Executive Officer | Chef de la direction,
Canadian Centre for Diversity and Inclusion
Toronto, Ontario, Canada

Acknowledgements

My family, my two daughters, and my brother and sister have been a constant source of support and love.

In addition, many others were instrumental in providing me with what I needed in order to successfully move forward to becoming my authentic self.

To my amazing editor, Diana Reyers, whose belief in the project and in me, along with her constant support, expertise, and determination made this memoir possible.

To my therapist, Deborah Hudson, who was literally a life saver over the two decades of support and friendship.

To my colleagues at Smith School of Business, David Saunders, Laurie Ross, and Michael Smith – a debt of gratitude for unquestioning acceptance and moving mountains to assist with my transition.

To all my friends at Trans Family Kingston and Kingston Pride, for their unwavering support and putting up with my occasional rants and frustration during my transition.

To Jean Pfleiderer and everyone in the Human Rights and Equity Office at Queen's University, thanks for your guidance and patience with my numerous questions and assurances that I was going to be okay.

Acknowledgements

To doctors Visram and Seidl, who do tremendous work assisting transgender people in the community and for making me feel safe and well cared for.

I am thankful for the assistance and support from Carla Brash, an overall amazing woman, my good friend and athletic therapist, and all her staff at her practice, who were invaluable in assisting with my physical recovery after my surgeries.

Thank you to Peter Jensen and the team at Third Factor Consulting, for constantly supporting me over the years and believing in me especially when I didn't. I knew I could always count on you to listen and remind me that I was valued. I am fortunate to have you and your family in my life.

To Kathleen Stevens, for being a part of my treatment team without hesitation or reservation and for the many long walks we had sharing what was going on in every aspect of our lives. Such a great friend then and now.

I would like to thank many others who supported and assisted me through my journey over the years. They are too many to mention in the space I have, however, you know who are.

And finally, to my fiancée and life partner, Julie, for her unwavering support and love. You constantly affirm who I am, my gender, my femininity, and sexuality. You are always there and make each day better. I look forward to laughing and sharing every aspect of our lives together for many years. No one has more fun than us!!

Prologue

By Erin Leeann LeBlanc

Life has struggles for the vast majority of us, and it seems, more for some than others. But, none the less, everyone has something they battle. The trick is to figure out how to get through the adversity and then find a way to control it within your life versus it controlling you. There is a saying, *That which doesn't kill you makes you stronger.* I disagree. I think that whatever doesn't kill you just really, really hurts, and you find a way to deal with it and work through it. It is then when you hopefully get stronger - hopefully. Sometimes, it feels like it is going to break you. So, how does one get to that point of tapping into their inner strength?

The story you are about to read is a narrative about what I went through and how I made it to the other side. It describes how I was pushed to my limits within my situation and experiences and how I almost broke. Almost. You will see that I was on the edge many times, but I always managed to step back from it and find the courage I needed to press on. Every time I tapped into resilience and was able to move forward just a bit more toward the confident, happy, strong woman I became to approach life and my future with enthusiasm. It is an account of my life from a young child to the present day. It is a recollection of events and feelings based upon anecdotes taken from my daily journal written from 2015 to 2018, which were some of my most traumatic times.

It was during this time when a culmination of forces truly tested my resolve and who I am at my core only to be able to emerge as a better person. Although I was moving through my transition, this is not just about that specific experience, but also encompasses the battles life threw at me and that I, simultaneously, fought at the time. You will see, I had to juggle many pieces at any one time. Fortunately, I have vividly written recordings in my journals that describe my thoughts and experiences during those years. I found it helpful to include some actual content to convey the genuine and raw emotions I felt within these impactful events. I hope this account will provide you with an understanding of how I felt within the trials and tribulations that are significant pieces of how I got to where I am today. To maintain the authenticity of my journal writings, they are transcribed in their original state and are not edited for grammar or spelling.

This is my interpretation of my story and how I saw it unfolding. While referencing feelings regarding my immediate family, including my now ex-wife, all my sharing is from my perspective. I do not know what anyone else's exact experience was then or is today. Even now, I have no idea what certain people exactly felt or thought through this journey because they never communicated how they felt to me. It is a recollection of my perceptions and perspectives, and as such, my reality. I am only able to provide my journey, and their story is for them to share if they want. This is not about them, it is just *my* story.

I intend to create a higher perspective as to what members of the LGBTQ+ community deal with, and in particular, the transgender community. While everyone's story is unique as their own, each may identify with specific themes, experiences, or emotions. I want you to know that you are not alone and that you are not the only one who has or is currently dealing with such feelings. My wish is that this memoir provides some degree of solace. For those who are supporting someone or are allies, this may help you to understand better what a person suffering from Gender Dysphoria and is transgender goes through. Likewise, if you are confused about your perception of this community or how to navigate supporting someone within it, my story may provide you with some clarity about what they might need from you. Never be afraid to ask them what they need and to have that conversation with them regardless of how uncomfortable it may feel. I found that everyone benefits in the end.

This is my memoir, a sharing of how I got to where I am today; how I moved from a disgruntled person to the confident, empowered, happy woman who sits here contemplating the past 60 years of her life. Yes, 60. I am what could graciously be called a *late bloomer*, and I will share several reasons for that as I go along through my story. It was later in life when I began to figure this all out, and more importantly, act upon it. But, at least I did. The fear of living a life filled with regret was almost more terrifying than not facing it at all. Being older doesn't make my experience less valid than those who are younger. I know the thoughts and feelings I share will resonant across generations when it comes to finding the path that is right for each of you. In my opinion, there is no way around it. To get to the other side, to not just survive but thrive, you must work your way through it and in your own way. Just as I did while climbing many hills, walking through some valleys, facing strong headwinds and horrific storms only to embrace the calm I was striving for eventually. I made it to the end of the journey, even though it hasn't come to the ultimate end yet. I don't think anyone's life path does. There is always something to work through to inspire our growth and be an even better person than we are today. For me, it still goes on as I continue to become more accepting of who I am and who I am meant to be while settling into my new and correct reality. Whether you are a member of the LGBTQ+ community, an ally, a family member, or a friend, I hope you find what I have, in some small way.

Let's begin, shall we?

Confusion

Journal Entry: June 7, 2016

The sense of relief is unbelievable. Done. Now I can focus on getting on with my life, doing my job, being with friends and family and continuing in my volunteer activities etc. The duality is gone. As we all know, this transition stuff is ridiculously some hard crap to wade through. Ask anybody who has done it and is completely full time in their correct gender. It sure as hell ain't for the faint of heart! I stopped keeping count of the times when it had knocked me down. But bloody and/or bruised, I somehow found the strength each time, to get back up, mostly due to the support of family and friends. However, I managed it, I did it. And it was so worth it! Every speed bump, detour, roadblock and occasional slip into a ditch made me a stronger person. Mine, like so many, if not all, was not an easy journey.

It's always difficult for me to try to figure out where to start. The obvious answer is *in the beginning*. For me, that's difficult to ascertain because where did it all begin? I know, for some who venture out on their journey to find their authentic self, they had a certain degree of clarity and understood their quest from a very early age. Many can actively recall memories from when they were very young, which included knowing they were not their correct gender. But, that was not the case for me.

In the famous words of Groucho Marx, *I must confess, I was born at a very early age.* I am the youngest of three, with a sister and brother. I know that I am physically the baby of the family, but in other ways, I feel I am not. There is somewhat of a gap between my brother and sister and me - eight and nine years, respectively. As a result, our maturity levels always varied at any given time while we were growing up, so we were never really close. Fortunately for me, that all changed with my transition.

Looking in from the outside, I had a happy childhood. But, having been on the inside, I know that was not the case. I have some memories that encompass occasions when I believe I experienced happiness. The catch is that when I look back on the narrative of my life, those instances were rooted in external activities and events, so I don't have any reflections of feeling happiness as an internal genesis. At the time, I didn't have any reason why; I just knew that something wasn't right, and I had no idea what was wrong. There was no internet or other sources of trustworthy, accurate, or reliable information readily available back then, so I just stumbled along.

Sitting here now, I see what transgender health specialists call *typical markers.* For instance, when I was little,

I wanted to wear pieces of clothing that are associated with the opposite of my sex assigned at birth, which was male - okay, there, I said it. Even now, speaking those words is extremely difficult for me as they trigger uncomfortable thoughts and emotions. I don't remember many details about the moments I resonated with what one describes as more feminine attire. Still, I certainly recall a sense of relief or inner peace when I was experiencing them. There were times like when I wore my mom's sweater at the age of five or six. Oh, how I loved the comfort and warmth of the soft fabric against my skin! The pleasant scent of womanhood that enveloped me provided such a great sense of calm. I understand the thought that this is normal, and every kid takes comfort in something that reminds them of their mom. But that was not it for me. No, I wanted to smell and feel like that. Even though I can articulate that now, I couldn't understand or internalize those feelings at that time. Not because I was ashamed of my reaction, but just because I was a child and couldn't logically figure it out. Instances like this happened over and over again, peppering my childhood and adolescence.

As a child and teenager, I had very few friends and didn't go out much. I had a difficult time relating to other kids. I didn't know who I was and didn't have a sense of how I was supposed to act around others. I was uncomfortable hanging out with groups of boys, and all I knew was that it didn't work for me. I recall my parents enrolling me in Boy Scouts, I guess, because my older brother was a Scout, and he did well. I made up so many excuses, so I didn't have to go to summer camp. The very thought of being surrounded by that many boys made me feel nauseous. We moved quite a bit due to my father's employment, and as a result, I went to seven different schools in eleven years. It got to the point when I didn't put much effort into making friends because I was afraid I would change schools again, so why bother? I am very clear that it in no way contributed to the dysphoria, but all these transient experiences certainly didn't help my situation, that's for sure! It just became another layer of stuff for me to work through.

I eventually became curious about girls, but in a different way than a typical teenage boy does. I was more fascinated by them as I watched how they moved, interacted, spoke, and dressed. I wanted to spend all my time with them instead of with boys. But of course, that was not going to happen because, in their eyes, any group of girls found that creepy, so I was not invited in by them. As a young person, I was confused as to what to do - I wasn't able to relate to boys, and girls didn't welcome me. I decided to fake it and tried to be a boy. When I look back, I see all the things that could go wrong with trying to be someone I wasn't and how that escalated throughout the years to come.

I tried participating in sports and doing what other boys did, and I was somewhat successful. My sport becoming varsity volleyball in junior high and high school, but the problem was that I hated every minute of it. It wasn't the sport I hated, but all the typical male rituals and hanging out with the *guys* that made me feel uncomfortable. I knew I could pull my weight because I was fast and nimble, but I wasn't big or strong, and there was way too much testosterone surging around within the group for my liking. The only saving grace is that we had a girls' team as well, and we travelled together to participate in tournaments. I remember feeling somewhat more balanced with them around. Of course, I didn't understand why, but I did feel more at ease.

I discovered much later in life that these are *typical markers* of someone who has Gender Dysphoria. I just had no idea what the heck was going on at the time. As I moved along in life, I continued to be super confused and suffered from depression, although not officially diagnosed until many years later.

I left for university with hopes of feeling better being away from a somewhat caustic environment at home and finding a place and a way to fit in. I was wrong. It was there where things went sideways for me. My academics suffered greatly, and once again, I was not able to cultivate any meaningful friendships. I had no social life because I somehow sabotaged any potential relationships with girls due to my low sense of self. I worked two part-time jobs, about 40 hours a week, to pay for tuition and bills because financial support from home was a non-starter.

I was essentially a mess, and I recognize now that it was all because of Gender Dysphoria. I had no idea that was the issue back then. I only see that now and wonder how I coped, and the answer is not well at all. I had to focus on one day at a time and find ways to be calm, which for the most part, meant being alone, so I didn't have to fake being happy while simultaneously warding off my anxiety about what others thought of me.

I think it became a case of being alone by myself versus feeling alone around others.

The former became my preferred survival technique because I didn't have to deal with the sense of being ignored, judged, or ridiculed by others. Granted, it wasn't the best strategy, but it was the only one I thought was an option at the time. I have thought about why I didn't seek help, counselling, or therapy, and I think the answer is mostly because I felt embarrassed about my situation. That may not be a reasonable thought, but I'm pretty sure I wasn't 100 percent rational at that time - just saying.

I had a major meltdown in my early 20's just after I managed to graduate. It was at that point I knew I had to get help. I called the medical helpline because I didn't have a regular family doctor, and they assigned one to me, so off I went. By this time, it was a bit easier for me to begin a discussion about what my problem was because I had recently lost weight without having been on a diet; I felt safe starting with that. As a result, I had several assessments done, and it quickly became apparent that my weight loss wasn't due to a physical medical issue, so I became more comfortable having discussions regarding my mental health. The doctors and I both knew something wasn't right, and of course, they wanted to figure what that was. During our conversations, it became clear I was experiencing confusion and a deep-seated lack of a sense of self-identity. As a result, they assessed me for schizophrenia, multiple personality disorder, bipolar disorder, and depression. Anything regarding Gender Dysphoria, as it is called today, was never part of the discussion. It wasn't even on their radar screen.

I felt there was a desperate desire by the doctors to label me, and they eventually placed a sticker of depression on my forehead. In their defense, that was accurate because I was depressed. As it turned out, I discovered years later that my Gender Dysphoria mostly caused the depression. They provided the option of either drug therapy or *talk therapy*. Not being one to rely on medication, I opted for the latter. The result was two and a half years of sessions with a therapist. Now, given everything I was experiencing, my dysphoria should have been easily spotted and correctly diagnosed for the first time in my life as something I was born with. But, that didn't happen, and I now admit that it was my fault.

I was in denial, big time. Nothing made sense to me. At this point, I had never heard of Gender Dysphoria or even had a therapist for that matter – I don't think many had back then. I was so confused. I was uncomfortable in the male persona, playing the typical male role, and I didn't understand why. Everyone around me, in particular men, seemed so sure of themselves, their role, and who they were while participating in typically male roles. For me, that was very confusing. I questioned it all. The environment I grew up in certainly didn't advocate that; males were men and females were women. Full stop! So, I was constantly in conflict with reminders to myself to suck it up. WTF! What the hell was the matter with me? My mandate became to get a hold of myself and *man up*. That evolved into my literal battle plan and my battle for life.

Fortunately for me, I met my saviour shortly after this. She is a kind and gentle soul who I loved very much, and I managed to convince her to marry me. Because I was abandoned so many times in my past, I took on a mission to make this relationship work. I experienced the feeling of being abandoned by my mom and dad. Any previous relationships I had with women left me feeling stranded, so I couldn't let that happen again. I tried super hard to be the man society expected me to be. And for the most part, I was able to do that. I was driven to make everyone around me happy. When they were happy, I was happy. And I was. I wasn't faking that.

For the next 20-plus years, any contentment I experienced, I generated externally. I fulfilled the expectation of being the typical role of a husband. Luckily for me, I became the father of two amazing daughters. At the time, this seemed to be enough. Experiencing life with my wonderful children felt like motivation enough to keep me going. This is what I thought until I came to learn first-hand, and with brutal reality, that Gender Dysphoria never goes away during pre-transition. It is something a person is born with. It doesn't respect any boundaries or strategies to keep it at bay. The unfortunate thing is that it is persistent, and when it breaks through, it is stronger than ever while increasing its intensity each time. That ain't any picnic!

To cope, I tried to find ways to fit in anywhere, including my family. For decades, even though I tried to find ways to create linkages where I could, I never felt I fit in or was welcome in a community. There were times when I tried to find a sense of belonging by gravitating towards physical items within my family. I tried to connect with personal belongings like furniture or small trinkets to create a sense of connection to something, but this didn't provide me with the feeling of truly fitting in. I then tried other strategies like doing the whole handyman thing attempting home and car repairs. Home renovations became a thing for me to focus on mostly because that is what guys stereotypically do. I went down that road of providing the outside world with what I believed they expected to see, which was a guy. But that wasn't working for me.

Most people attain a sense of accomplishment or pride when completing DIY projects, but I didn't. I hated doing all that stuff. I was only doing them because it was part of my strategy. Right or wrong, it was part of my plan to feel like I belonged to others, especially to my family. The problem was that the more I tried, the more my plan failed, and this became an ugly downward spiral. The more things I tried that didn't work, the more isolated, different, and out of control I felt. It was like floating out into space with no home, no real sense of who I was. I became lost as to what to do.

I quickly found a therapist, and that's when things finally began getting a bit clearer. I went to see my family doctor, who referred me to one who was well versed in gender issues. By that time, the world of medicine had caught up with the *condition* and the symptoms associated with it. I owe my therapist such a huge debt of gratitude because, over the next 17 years, she literally talked me off so many ledges as my lifesaver. Within several sessions, she confirmed I had Gender Dysphoria or Gender Identity Disorder as it was called at that time. I was now in my late 30s.

In one sense, it was a great relief. A relief because someone finally understood what I was born with and what I was going through. But in another sense, I was terrified of reaching the realization that I was not the gender I was born to be. I was born a woman and had fought that for decades. This was an education for me; to realize that this was something outside of my control and that I couldn't just will it away. I came into the world with this, and I recall thinking at the time that the good news is that I am transgender. But, at the same time, the bad news is that I am transgender! I was completely scared to death. Initially, I didn't fully understand what all this meant, but through additional sessions over a few years, I came to realize exactly what it meant for me.

Here's the trick. At the time, I wasn't prepared to pay the price required to fulfill who I was in order to transition. And my therapist agreed. She stated, quite ardently, that it wasn't my time because I wasn't ready to transition yet. She told me I wasn't ready emotionally, mentally, or financially. And my family wasn't ready either. She also brought my work into the scenario and told me it wasn't ready. Finally, she indicated that the whole of society wasn't ready, and with certainty, the world of medicine wasn't ready. She said that if I truly wanted to go ahead, she would help me through it, but she felt it was a terrible bad idea - a really, really bad idea, given the current situation. So, with all that in mind, I decided not to act on the diagnosis.

I felt I was strong enough to fight off transition, and I was motivated to keep my marriage and family intact. That was definitely the number one priority for me. It wasn't even a matter up for debate, and I committed to this decision to the point of self-destruction.

We decided to work out a plan to keep me going while creating strategies to try to keep a lid on the secret I was keeping with hopes those strategies would get me through it all. Well, as they say, the best-laid plans.

Most of the plans we decided on did not work. I think because I wasn't in any headspace to make any of them work. One of the things I was supposed to do was fully celebrate things, like birthdays, Christmas and Thanksgiving, to focus on those happy times. Okay, sure. Why not? Well, here's the thing, I didn't have a problem celebrating other people's birthdays... not at all. I'm all in, let's make it a great time. But mine, not so much. Internally, I was unable to get on board with it no matter what I did. I discovered this was due to a deep sense of not feeling deserving of celebrating the recognition of my birth. What was there to celebrate? I often wondered why I was even born. The same feelings surfaced with Christmas, that feeling that I wasn't deserving of receiving gifts and all that goes along with this special day. It sounds ridiculous, but not for someone suffering from Gender Dysphoria. That's how dark it got.

With that, I'm going to back up a bit. Not time-wise, but in order to explain what my medical diagnosis means. When I do presentations to groups, I inevitably get questions regarding the whole notion of gender. Gender Identity Disorder (GID), first listed as a medical condition in 1980, was more accurately renamed as Gender Dysphoria in 2010.The first thing to consider is what physical sex as assigned at birth actually means. Essentially, it is the sex someone is labelled with at birth solely based on physical characteristics. So, if born with a penis, one is assigned the physical sex of a male. If born with a vagina, one is assigned the physical sex of a female. That's pretty straight forward. However, here's the rub. Physical sex is not the same as gender. That is what one identifies as in their brain, heart, and soul. In a sense, the very essence that is you. Furthermore, the connection between physical sex assigned at birth and gender is not 100 percent written in stone. That is to say, your sex and gender can be different.

During gestation, physical sex is determined first, and in my case, that was male. At some point, gender is determined, and mine is female. I am not an expert in any way, shape, or form, however, what I do know is that my brain was pre-wired to accept estrogen, that is to say, my gender is as a woman. However, my body was a testosterone-producing machine with my brain, simultaneously craving estrogen. Hence, my brain wasn't pleased with my physical self. My sex did not match my gender. There was nothing anyone could do about it. It was totally out of my control. No amount of wishing it away or psychotherapy could help. I constantly battled this for over five decades with the result of living with dysphoria. I admit that this is an over-simplistic introduction to the definition of the terms and the condition, but it should suffice for this monograph.

Simply put, this is not a choice. I can't count how many times I heard the absolute ridiculous statement that being transgender is a lifestyle choice. A choice? Oh, please! Seriously? Oh my gosh. I wouldn't wish Gender Dysphoria on my worst enemy. It is an awful, soul-sucking, debilitating condition that disables any strong sense of who you are. A choice? I don't think so. There is such an agonizing commitment to the time, energy, and emotional and physical suffering dedicated to hours of therapy, medical appointments, hormone treatments, not to mention, laser treatments and electrolysis for facial hair removal for male to female (MtF) transgender women. I can attest that facial electrolysis is no picnic! For me, it took two years of weekly appointments, zapping every hair one at a time. And each hair has to be hit about five times to make sure the root is dead. It felt like plucking a nose hair out 100 times every week for two years. A choice? No. I did not choose this.

This is what it is like when deciding to transition, and only when having the support and resources to do it. So, it is little wonder that the suicide attempt rate for those born with Gender Dysphoria is about 40% in North America, according to a study done by the Williams Institute, UCLA, 2014.[1] The most cited causes were being abandoned by family (57%), experiencing harassment at work (59%), and the refusal of medical treatment to begin transitioning (60%). These numbers apply just to those who attempted suicide. The number of trans people who thought about suicide is ridiculously high. And for all the same reasons... fear.

I totally understand that. I was scared to death about what my future was going to be like. I wondered if my family would abandon me, my wife, daughters, sister, brother, and other family members? Would I still be employed, have friends, be welcome in my neighbourhood, or would I be forced to move out? This list goes on, and on, and on, and it was terrifying. Simply terrifying.

This was all part of the discussion with my therapist which lead to my decision to, initially, not transition and to fight it. I tried. I really did. I tried my best to do the man thing. I did what so many in my transgender community do by compensating - big time. Self-denial continued to rule, and I over-compensated; anything to fight it. Many in the LGBTQ community, particularly males, over-compensate by engaging in dramatic male roles and activities like enlisting in the military, law enforcement, fire and rescue services, anything that is typically rich with testosterone. I did this as well to a certain degree. I already had a career, so I needed some type of hobby or past-time to try to trick my brain and make me feel like the majority of males.

I chose scuba diving. It was something I truly enjoyed,

[1]Herman, J., Brown, T., Haas, A. (2019) Suicide Thoughts and Attempts Among Transgender Adults: Findings from the 2015 U.S. Transgender Survey, Research that Matters UCLA School of Law, Williams Institute, pp1-3.

and quite frankly, I was good at it. The bonus about choosing scuba diving is that my two daughters were also interested in it. So, we took courses and got certified. It was something we had in common and that we all enjoyed. To set the record straight in reference to my girls, I was genuinely happy around them. When I was with them from the time they were born and watching them grow up, I experienced deep joy. The trick was that my emotional wellness depended on them. Although I was grateful for that gift, I realized I was back to where I started because I fed off their happiness which was generated externally. None of my joy came from within me.

This is all part of Gender Dysphoria. Ain't it grand?! It's something most people don't understand - that when someone is born with Gender Dysphoria, they are not in control. The condition is fully in the driver's seat. I was simply a passenger on the bus travelling along in my life, and it was an awful, horrible feeling. To be that much out of control of my life every day was like having a stranger looking at me in the mirror, constantly taunting me.

What is so *macho* about scuba diving? Actually, not much. Thankfully, these days there are so many women enjoying the sport. But I decided to take it up a notch. The dive team I was associated with was all military and trained at the local military base in my city; no testosterone there!!! I committed to my training, moving up to advanced diving, becoming a rescue diver, ice diver, all the way up to divemaster. I volunteered to be a safety diver at local events in support of my city police. I also assisted in training divers to dive under the ice. I desperately tried to be the man I was expected to be within scuba diving. And, that worked for a bit. But over a period of time, that wasn't enough.

The dysphoria came and went, but each time it came back stronger and stronger. Even when I managed to beat it back with sheer willpower, I knew deep down it wasn't going to be enough. I knew it would be back. There was nothing I could do about it. Feeling helpless, I now see how easy it was for depression to find a cozy home within me. Which it did.

Then things started to go sideways - even more sideways than usual. To the point that it was truly frightening. Even with the strategies my therapist gave me, it was a terrifying time. I tried grounding exercises, being mindful, and staying *in the now* practices and routines, but nothing worked. It was an extremely hard time culminating in a singular event that was somewhat of a turning point...

Desperation

The critical event occurred when I was on my own, out of town at a conference. I didn't write in my journal that night that I was scared. Really scared. I didn't know what to do as I sobbed uncontrollably and was in no shape to drive home. No one there knew about me, so there was no one I could call. I thought about calling 9-1-1, but wondered, what could they do? It was the first time I was that scared, and others followed. I don't know what I would have done if Erin didn't show up. But she did… and she literally saved me.

I attempted to practice a grounding exercise provided by my therapist in response to my crippling mental state. It requires getting into the most comfortable position possible, relaxing and tracking my breathing - deep breaths, focusing my mind on opening the door to my heart and my soul in an attempt to reach my core and get grounded, focusing on the now. I did that, and it was a bit of a breakthrough.

February 6, 2016

Hey, it's me...

Yesterday, my mind was totally embroiled about a conversation I had with myself on Friday, October 23, 2014. How do I know that date you ask? Well, that was the day I had a really bad meltdown. Maybe breakdown is the best way to describe it.

So, here's the setting. October 2014, I was at a conference, representing an organization I volunteer at as Chair of the Board of Governors. Made it through the day but was tired as I always was back then as I was presenting as male which was exhausting. Trying to relax, I was soaking in the tub practicing some mindfulness exercises my therapist taught me to try to focus and get grounded again. To look into your heart and just be. Well, that's when I completely lost it. Totally inconsolable, not sure what I was going to do, a three hour drive from home at a remote resort, my mind was totally spinning. So, tried to get grounded and FAST! That's when the conversation started with the voice in my heart.

Voice: *Hey...*

Me: *What?*

Voice: *Hey...it's me.*

Me: *Okay...?*

Voice: *It's me. I can help.*

Me: *Whattaya mean, you can help?*

Voice: *I can help. Just let me. Just let me out.*

Me: *Out?*

Voice: *Ya, Out.*

Me: *What? How? Why?*

Voice: *Look...all this pain, despair, suffering you have been going through? I can help. Just let me help you!*

Me: *How? Who are...?*

Voice: *It's me. Erin*

Me: *Erin?*

Voice: *Yes. Erin. Let me out. Show the world who you really are. Let me out and all of this will get better.*

Me: *Better?*

Voice: *Yes.... you, dumb ass! You know who you are. Time to do it babe. It's time. It's your time. Time to drop the facade, the lies, the acting. Be who you were meant to be... your authentic self.*

Me: *Oh, that's all!*

Voice: *Yes, that's all ! Good lord. Trust me. I am who you are. Let me out. It's the only way to get passed all of this. Stop denying it. Stop fighting it. All you have to do is be you.*

Me: *Uh-huh. Not so easy....my whole life....puff....gone!*

Voice: *You don't know that. You may be surprised at all the support you will have to become you. And, it's better than the alternative.*

Me: *Alternative?*

Voice: *Yes. I guarantee, if you don't do this, then ya, it will be puff.... gone, if you know what I mean! Don't deny every one of your beauty and kindness and wisdom and love. Just let me out.*

Me: *Erin......?*

Voice: *Ya, Babe*

Me: *I can't go on. I'm not sure I have what it takes.*

Voice: *Yes, you do. You do if you let me help. Just let go. Just be who you are. That's it. I'm here. I'm strong. I will survive. You've got to do this.*

Me: *Let me think about it? There's a lot to think about. There's a lot of people this impacts.*

Voice: *Yes, true. It does. Let me just say that it's time to put you first. You've got this. Remember, I'm here, ready to go. I always will be. I've been with you since you were born and I'm not going anywhere. And, that's when I think I fell asleep. I remember all of this like it was yesterday. I'm pretty sure this conversation is only a modification of what everyone goes through at some point in their journey to become their true self. I'm here to say, listen to that inner voice from your heart. It's okay. I'm so glad that I eventually made the decision. It took a few more conversations, because, well, let's just say, I can be a bit slow on the uptake sometimes.*

It's that inner strength that we all have. It's there for you like it was and still is, for me. It's who you are. Just allow yourself to be you. It's a lot less energy than all the acting we've all done through the decades of our life.

The voices or discussion I had was not in my head. I didn't hear voices, but rather, the voices were in my heart. And, the message conveyed was a feeling created from my core being so I wasn't concerned that I was going mad or that I was schizophrenic or had multiple personalities. It was just a feeling of getting in touch with my true self that came over me. I know many resonate with the yearning to connect with their authentic self. But for most, it's likely a general inner struggle, rather than the dilemma of their sex being opposite of their gender.

The sad thing is that I'm pretty sure everyone who has Gender Dysphoria to this extent finds themselves in a similar circumstance. And there are those whose inner *Erin* doesn't show up. It's understandable why the attempted suicide rate is 43% in my more immediate community.[2] And in my experience, the general public doesn't want to hear such things. And yet, they need to listen to it.

---

[2]"Suicidality among trans people in Ontario: Implications for social work and social justice" Greta R. Bauer, Jake Pyne, Matt Caron Francino et Rebecca Hammond, Service social, vol. 59, n° 1, 2013, p. 39

People need to know how serious Gender Dysphoria is.
This is not a game.
This is not a choice.
This is a terrible way to go through life.

The time came for me to choose a name. Not many get to pick their name, and while it's cool to think about, it's also quite a daunting task. At least it could be. It was not so much for me. I was lucky because I always knew I was Erin. That was never up for debate because that name was simply who I am. I didn't even have to think about it; I just knew that was my name. It instantly came from somewhere deep inside my heart and my soul. There was no trying out different names because it was a done deal. Perhaps that was the reason She was so strong within me - Erin is who I am.

That left the middle and last names. As to the latter, that was a no-brainer because it stayed the same. It wasn't because I was attached to it, I don't feel wedded to it. If my sex would have matched my gender and I was born the woman I am now, I'm pretty sure I would change my last name if I married, especially if the process weren't such a pain in the butt. But I digress. The reason I kept my last name was to honour my daughters. For them to have any connection to who I am is important to me. I hope this provides them with some sense of comfort. Ironically, they could very well change their last name when they get married, but that will be their choice, not mine.

Now, as for my middle name, well, that was a different story. I knew it had to change, so I had to pick one. I decided it needed to be the name I would have received if assigned my correct gender at birth. This is something that many in my community do when choosing a name, and I resonated with it in order to honour the wishes of my parents. It would maintain a tie to them, and I felt that would be amazing. But, my first name was set; I am Erin. Done deal. So, I decided I would honour them with my middle name.

Because my mother had just passed away, I finally took the opportunity to have this discussion with my father. I simply asked him outright if he knew what I would have been called if I was a girl. Without any hesitation, he said, no, he had no idea. Since my parents would have been the ones to name me if I was born a girl, and neither could, I began the process of deciding what my middle name would be on my own. I still wanted to maintain some tie to my family, so I started running down a list of relative's names. Being of French descent, many of the names just didn't resonate with me. And many definitely didn't sound good with Erin.

I looked at my sister's names, as well as my sister-in-law's. It's not uncommon in French culture for family members to share a middle name, and most have two middle names. However, I didn't want to do that. I felt that one middle name was more than sufficient. Considering all that, I came up with Elizabeth. Erin Elizabeth. I liked the way it rolled off my tongue. The one sticky point is that my initials would be E.E.L. Hmmm, not so good. But, not the worst thing either, so I settled on that.

Then one day on a whim, I decided to ask my sister if she knew what our parents were going to call me if I was a girl. Just like my father, she replied without a moment's hesitation. However, her response was, Yes, it was going to be Leeann. Seriously?! What the hell?! She would have been nine at the time, so if she remembered, I wondered why my dad didn't. Something was going on there, but I decided to pick my battles at this point, and this wouldn't be one of them.

I loved the name, absolutely loved the name!! It was my

name! And there it was, Erin Leeann. I was fortunate that I had not begun what proved to be the arduous task of registering my name change yet. It wasn't too late as there was nothing to be undone. It took about a year to eventually go through the entire name change process before it finally became official.

So, that is the beautiful story of how my new name was birthed, along with the major epiphany that inner Erin was there to help and guide me, but this was by no means the end to my inner turmoil.

January 3, 2015

When I look in the mirror in DRAB - Dressed As a Boy - I don't see anything special or someone who I can love or can be loved. And, I hate looking in mirrors BTW. But when I picture myself as my true self, Erin, I see someone I do love, can be loved, has something to contribute, is positive and fun. None of which I see in my male self.

January 3, 2015

Presenting male gets me depressed, so I get very quiet, not smiling a lot, or engaged. Which really sucks, especially for my wife. She deserves so much more.

For years, this was how I constantly felt. I'm pretty sure it's a prevalent feeling for pre-transition transgender people, which sucks. And, it sucked for me during this time while presenting as male when things were pretty bad because I knew it wasn't just impacting me.

And this did not go away. In fact, instead of getting better, things continued to get worse. I continued to have anxiety attacks, and they got progressively more frequent and intense.

At one point during this time, they became close to debilitating. They most often occurred at work, which became quite difficult, with the trigger being the slightest thing catching me completely off guard. I worked through them most of the time, but quite often, they came on fast and strong, and I couldn't keep it together. It was during these times when I quickly found a quiet place to sit and allowed the anxiety to pass. The good news is that they usually didn't last more than ten minutes and even less if I found the strength to push through them. It was the strong ones that usually resulted in tears and a very deep sense of desperation.

It may be difficult to understand for those not suffering from Gender Dysphoria, but my life encompassed this kind of suffering. All it took to trigger this anxious state was to see something or someone who I desperately wanted to have or be like. It always had something to do with women like hairstyle, makeup, facial features, body shape, or clothing, movement, scent, stature, or confidence. I could go on and on. That is how much this controlled my life. Being transgender a choice? Nope, I don't think so.

With the help of my therapist, I decided to implement a strategy to help me deal with this. One of my biggest triggers was facial hair, so I decided to see what I could do about that. I discovered that laser treatments can eliminate dark hair but not light hair. Even though my hair was starting to turn grey, I'm fortunate I had dark facial hair. The trick was to find a laser treatment centre that was *trans-friendly*. That wasn't necessarily the easiest thing to do in my community. For whatever reason, many companies in the service industry don't want to deal with transgender people. I learned to be completely upfront with any service provider I called. I found it was better to find out right at the start, so I wasn't wasting my time. The good news is that while there were only a few laser centres where I lived, one was recommended to me that had technicians with experience working with transgender people. At first, I thought this would be the end of facial hair being a trigger for me. Nope, not even close. It took a year of monthly treatments of my entire face to get rid of just the dark hair, and then there was the issue of what to do about the grey hair, which happened later.

This was one strategy that worked for me, but things continued getting worse. I was able to fight back the intensity of my internal battle for quite some time, but it continued to manifest and build, and I know I was not a very pleasant person. But I didn't know how to make that go away.

January 17, 2015

Ever have one of those days?! Well, I have. I am so angry and frustrated and sad, and I don't know why. Okay, so that is a bold-faced lie. It is because I have a male body. Duh! I guess what I mean is that there is nothing really that happened today specifically that had caused this. But if life had a face, I would punch it!

If I'm honest, I did know how to make it all go away - I think I did deep down. It became obvious I had to balance my brain through Hormone Replacement Therapy. At the very least, I knew this had to happen. I needed to get rid of the testosterone that was poisoning my brain and get some estrogen in there. It is estrogen that my brain was pre-wired to receive at birth, and it wasn't getting any. But I was still in denial. Big time. Looking back, I kept trying to *man up*; it's almost comical to think I could do that, and it would be that easy.

I found myself developing a little rating system to mentally keep track of how I was doing and how my day was going. It sounds really ridiculous and overly dramatic now when I think about it, but for some reason, it seemed appropriate at the time. In my mind, I had a six-shooter with an empty cylinder -the place where the bullets go. Every time I experienced something that *triggered* my dysphoria, I mentally put a bullet in one of the six chambers. I guess maybe the idea of a trigger lead me to the analogy of a gun.

This system allowed me to measure how my day was going; the more bullets, the greater the likelihood of an anxiety attack. I felt I might be able to catch the attack early and manage it by tracking the number of bullets I put in as I went along. In my mind, a 3-bullet-day was my new normal - 4 was a bit alarming, and 5 was reason to take a step back. A 6-bullet-day was definitely not good.

For about six months, my typical day began with me taking trigger inventory. I looked in the mirror and saw that stupid, ugly male face that needed shaving. Trigger. One bullet in the chamber. I then went through the activity of shaving. Trigger. Second bullet in the chamber. Next, I got dressed in clothing appropriate for a man. Trigger. Third bullet in the chamber. So, the start of my day began with three bullets out of six in the chamber. That didn't leave a lot of room for anything else to pop up during the rest of the day.

When I speak to groups about my experiences, I often ask the women in the audience how they feel about this. I ask them how they would feel if they had to start their day seeing enough facial hair that they feel the need to remove it and then go through the actual act of shaving. Some have a hard time relating to Gender Dysphoria because they have always experienced congruity between their sex and gender.

This little exercise brings them the awareness of imagining life without that congruity.

I started to think more and more about my need to transition. I wondered if this was the path I wanted to take. The cost was going to be very high, so I bloody well better be sure. 1000 percent sure.

January 21, 2015

I know that this journey is never going to be straight forward. There will be detours and obstacles along the way. I am going to have to get used to hearing that irritating voice saying "recalculating".

I began digging deeper to determine how I could be sure and received some insight from my therapist. She told me she had taken me as far as she could. She was confident what my path should be, but she wasn't the one to a) make that call and b) be the one to get me there. She recommended I find a therapist who specializes in Gender Dysphoria, and I wondered out loud if there was even such a thing. Trust me, she said, there is. That was good enough for me because, for the previous seventeen years, I trusted this woman with my very life. The trick was to find one who was taking new patients.

I also needed to find an endocrinologist, the best person to discuss the possibility of starting Hormone Replacement Therapy (HRT) for dosages of testosterone blockers and estrogen, ongoing monitoring of blood work, blood pressure, and overall general physical health. This proved to be easier said than done, and in the meantime, life continued. Sometimes, that wasn't such a good thing.

January 23, 2015

Well, I had a bit of a moment last night. For some reason, this whole thing came crashing down on me in an emotional wave. I got really scared of all of this, kept wondering how I am going to do it, I can't do this by myself. I sat on the edge of the bed and sobbed for about twenty minutes. When it was all over, I felt a bit better, but the thought of having to do this all by myself still resides. I think in my heart, though I feel so alone, I can do it, I am pretty strong, but in my brain, not so much.

I decided I needed to keep moving, and that's what I kept trying to do. The fact that I'm a planner often helped me. It's what I do, and sometimes it's a curse while other times it supports me. In this case, it helped me focus on the positive and move forward because if I took my eye off the road ahead, wham, I spun out of control.

So, in hopes of keeping my vehicle that is my life between the guardrails, I plan.

The search for both a gender therapist and an endocrinologist continued. At the time, there were seven endocrinologists in my city. None of them, not one, would see a transgender patient. Seriously?! WTF. I felt I wasn't worthy of their time or attention, and yet, I wasn't any different than any of their other patients needing support balancing my hormones, plain and simple. However, the stigma of being transgender is still a thing within the medical profession. As ridiculous as this is, I needed to get used to it and move forward. But there was an issue – I began hesitating and rethinking if I was sure this was the route I wanted to take.

I came to the realization that *wanted* is not the right word and needed made more sense to me. I asked myself, *Is this the journey I need to take?* I had to believe my life would be better once arriving on the other side of my transition.

Despite these thoughts, things took a bit of a turn for the worst. Despite all the work I did and all the strategies I continued to employ to keep my head above water, things went to an alarming state of affairs fast. I mean really fast. These are the perils of living with debilitating Gender Dysphoria. These are the ups and downs I experienced, thinking I could beat it back one minute and then the next minute finding myself trying to figure out how to accept it and move forward.

I remember the following incident quite vividly. It was a clear, cold Saturday morning in February, and I was on my way to my favourite dive shop to chat with the owner, who is a friend of mine. I wanted to check out what was new in the world of scuba diving. I chose to take the scenic route instead of the highway because it was much more pleasant following the shoreline for the majority of the drive. Water is very comforting to me, so taking the shoreline road was a bit of a treat.

The entire time I drove, I asked myself why I was doing this. I wondered why I was going to the dive shop, putting myself in the man cave that was the sacred place of all testosterone. I knew deep down that nothing good could come of this, but I also knew the answer was that I was a man, and this is what men do. I was engaging in total resistance to what I needed to do. I was in complete denial of being this thing called transgender. I dove into the mental torture that goes with Gender Dysphoria. This was not a choice because there is no way anyone would choose the fast downward spiral I was about to go on. My mind quickly went to a really stupid place, so quickly that no amount of reasoning would have any positive impact. At least not in those two or three minutes.

I convinced myself I couldn't do this and that life wasn't worth it. At that same moment, I saw an oncoming snowplow, which is a typical site in February where I lived. *That'll do*, I said, *He's big and won't cause any harm to the driver. All I have to do is clip the plow, take out my driver's side, and it will be done. I will have peace at last.* I had about ten seconds before he was on me. One quick turn of the wheel, and it would be over. The countdown was on, 10 – 9 – 8… And then suddenly, for whatever reason, I turned the wheel back at the very last nano-second and blew passed him. I pulled the car over at the first safe spot I could find. I was shaking and turned off the engine. I took the key out of the ignition and threw it in the back of the car. Then, I broke down and cried for about 20 minutes. Oh, how I cried.

Finally, the shaking stopped, and I had no more tears to cry. What just happened? Why didn't I do it? Erin - that's what just happened. Once again, it was the voice from my heart, my very soul that broke through and took over. It was the will to survive, her will to survive that was stronger. And thank goodness it was. I managed to collect myself, get back home, and took a deep breath going through the rest of the day as if nothing happened. Once again, I went back to donning the mask that was the façade of being male.

Fortunately, I had an appointment with my regular therapist the week following my *episode* for lack of a better term. We discussed being safe, moving forward. It was very apparent what needed to be done, and she quite succinctly stated the obvious, even to me.

It's your time. You've got to go. You're ready. With the proper guidance, you will be prepared, and emotionally and mentally, you need to do this. Financially, you're ready. Your workplace is ready. Society is ready. The medical world is ready. It won't be easy and yes some family may not be with you at the end, but this is your time.

If I had to pick a time when I realized I knew without a doubt and accepted I had to transition to survive, this was it. It was frightening and liberating all at the same time. I was terrified thinking about what it all meant. I knew what was going to happen and what could potentially happen in my life. I knew I was going to lose my wife, a wonderful person. I knew I could potentially lose my girls, my family, friends, employment, and any connections I had to a community. As a result of these revelations, there were times when I was not able to keep it together - at all. I cried every day. EVERY day. And the fun part - not - is that I never really knew when it was going to hit. So that became tricky, often needing to find a private place, whether at work or home, to deal with it. This usually took twenty minutes or so in order to get it together enough to get through the day.

It most often happened at home, and usually when I just got home seeing my wife as I walked through the door. It was devastating for me to deal with the realization that I knew I was going to hurt someone. Something else that provoked me was thinking about everything I was going to lose, the prospect of losing my home and everything we built together as a family. All this manifested inside of me to the degree that I often found myself sobbing while alone doing tasks like preparing dinner.

Of course, it goes without saying, I worried terribly about

the impact all this would have on my girls. I tried so hard, so very hard, to be the father they needed. I was completely driven to do whatever it took to make them happy and for them to feel loved, valued, and supported. The bonus for me was that if they were happy, I was happy. Over the years, that's how I got through a lot of this. But at this awful time, not even that could console me. Everyone in my family deserved so much better and so much more than what I was able to give them.

Pile on the deep-seated feeling of failing as a man, not just as a father but as a husband, I'm ashamed to say I took this out on my wife. I got upset when asked to do things like repairing something or if she pointed out that something needed fixing, and there was one incident when I almost completely lost it.

Sadness

The kitchen faucet was leaking, it was just a leaky faucet! That's all it was. Are you kidding me? Nope, that was it - a simple thing like a faucet that was dripping.

March 2, 2015

Why do women think men should be able to fix stuff? Come to the rescue? What is it with that?? I hate, HATE, working with tools and doing any type of repairs or renovations. I suck at it. I don't like it. And I don't do it. That is why they have tradespeople. I like to think that I create employment and stimulate the economy by hiring these talented folk to do the voodoo that they do so well (to coin a phrase...)

It is expectations/stereotyping like that, that just pisses me off sometimes. And I guess, at some level, reinforces that I am a failure as a male. Which on the one hand bothers me, but on the other, just reinforces that I need to be the real me. The world is just going to have to get used to that. The real me is not who I am now...

For all of that, I am truly sorry.

Now, don't get me wrong; I did some work around house renovations and other jobs. Mostly because that's what real men do, and I was trying to convince myself that I was a real man. That was me, always in a constant state of self-denial. That ended up not being what it's cracked up to be as it led me to complete feelings of unworthiness, insecurity, and a low sense of value. On top of all that, I hated doing these manly tasks. I painted, installed hardwood floors, built decks, took out walls, and renovated the kitchen and two bathrooms. All the while HATING every moment of it. I mean I really hated it all. Some people experience a sense of accomplishment by doing things like this themselves, but that was not me. Nope. Zero. Nada. Not part of my DNA...literally.

But I did them because it made other people happy, most importantly, my wife and daughters. I wasn't happy, so making those I loved happy became my full-time job. There was a bit of catch because I thought that all that joy would naturally transfer onto me as well. However, although my family's happiness did provide me with a level of contentment, I discovered long before being diagnosed with Gender Dysphoria that if I didn't accept who I was in my own skin as the person I am, I could not be truly happy. However, at this point, I decided my wife and kids were going to have a happy life, even if it killed me. Okay, that's an unfortunate choice of words.

I believe I also wanted to feel I was contributing to these

relationships somehow. I wanted to provide some kind of value. There had to be a reason for them to keep me around, so I hoped these overt acts would provide some evidence of it because I did not feel it internalized within me. Hence, I had what was validated by others who knew me and can be described as an eager to please mentality. This eventually became quite exhausting.

I also had to work really hard on strategies to not only cope but also keep myself safe. This is something I developed with the help of my therapists. I quickly realized that one thing I had to do was stop scuba diving. This was unfortunate because it was something I enjoyed for whatever reason, and I also found some sense of peace within it. Saying that, even with the proper training and experience I had under my belt, there were circumstances around it within which I could not put myself through anymore.

March 15, 2015

Interesting self-realization today…

I was to participate in an "ice dive" with my team today. Sort of a "keep up the skills" event and a bit of fun. Ice was 28 inches thick. The hole we cut was 6 feet by 3 feet. Water temperature was 32.5F. Visibility under the ice at 80 feet. But I just couldn't bring myself to do it. Which for me is really odd. So, I stayed on the surface with the rest of the support team, emergency divers, etc., to help out as surface support. It was good to still be involved.

But the realization I came to was that I just couldn't trust myself to keep myself safe. You have to be on your "A" game in these situations. To be able to respond should something go sideways, and in that environment, it often can. But mentally, it is taking all I have just to "keep it together" in the best of situations. This GD is taking its toll on me mentally. It is exhausting for me. My training would have probably kicked in should something have happened, but I didn't trust that I had what it took mentally to keep myself safe under there.

I just couldn't bring myself to slip under the ice. It terrified me, which has never, ever happened regardless of when or where I have been diving. From 150 feet down, 5 levels down in the bowels of a battleship in the South Pacific, to visibility of 2 feet or less in a lake. Nothing bothered me. But today…oh brother…it was not good.

My takeaway from this is that my "self-preservation" instinct kicked in and is stronger than the "dark side", so I am taking this as a good sign…stay out of harm's way.

This experience provided the awareness that I needed to think about my mindset at that time. I was a bit more convinced of what my destiny would be, and the search for a gender therapist was now in high gear. I still wanted to be absolutely sure this was what I needed to do and the path I was meant to take. I wasn't going to blow up my life on a whim, but blow it up, I did.

I remember the day it happened as if it was yesterday. As I say it, that sounds quite cliché, but it feels like the best way. I was miserable for quite some time - basically, ever since my brush with death. Regretfully, it was probably even worse for my wife. I'm not making an excuse, but I really couldn't help myself. I was tired…exhausted really, tired of everything. Tired of being me, or more accurately, not being me. Trying to keep it together was exhausting. I was simply going through the motions getting up each morning at 6:30, staring at the stupid ugly face in the mirror, going out into the freezing cold to walk my pup, and dealing with, what I felt at the time was the incessant ridiculous banter of my neighbours in the dark. I hated the cold and snow as I still do, and all of this was an additional strain on my psyche.

Work was okay, but not great. I had anxiety attacks that showed up out of the blue, which made me somewhat unpredictable - not so much to others but to myself. I was essentially on pins and needles, not knowing when I might suffer one.

For anyone who has never experienced an anxiety attack, "suffer" is not too strong a word.

I spent the greatest amount of what little energy I had keeping up a reasonable façade while doing my job and participating in meetings when I had to. Other than that, I tried keeping to myself and under no circumstances did I look in a mirror.

By the end of each day, I was emotionally vacant - done. But, unfortunately, my day wasn't over. On a typical day, I got home, usually the first to arrive, and took my pup for another walk in what was still the freezing cold – a typical February and March in Canada! After getting back from the walk, I thought about what to make for dinner. Not much went on in the evenings. I was spent and had nothing left to offer or contribute, and I hated that. There's no other way to describe it, I hated the way I felt.

At some point, not long after dinner, I would decide to go to bed. I needed quiet and dark. I also wanted to give my wife time to be away from me. I didn't feel I was worthy of being around. Thank you, Gender Dysphoria! The hope was that I would somehow get to sleep before my wife came to bed. I don't often dream, but I found myself hoping I would as I tried to get to sleep; my wish was that my dreams would bring me to a better place. I longed to be in a place where I wasn't in the despicable shell of a body that was me. Other than the fact I had two amazing daughters, I didn't have much to show for my life. If it wasn't for them, I often thought the world would be better off if I hadn't been born. I believed I provided no value. Looking back, it's not a surprise I ended up in a dark place with that noodling around in my head for years. More often than not, I ended up crying myself to sleep as exhaustion eventually set in. All this, only to repeat every moment the next day. Welcome to my *Groundhog Day*.

I can honestly say that it wasn't total doom and gloom. There were some good days, the ones when I was able to fight the dysphoria and keep a lid on things. There were days when I was happy. Whether I was a happy person to be with is not my story to tell. But, there were some fun times, mostly because of my family, my wife, and my daughters. I mean, I did have a good life, a good job, a great family, and a nice house. I can see that someone not suffering from Gender Dysphoria would feel that's enough to last a lifetime! But that's exactly what dysphoria robs you of, and in the majority of cases, it takes over your family, your job, friends, and even your home. Again, I don't know too many people who would be crazy enough to choose this. Nope. Sorry. This is not a lifestyle choice. Not even close. It is about survival, plain and simple.

So, this was our life, such as it was. And it became clear to me that our relationship had reached a breaking point. I felt the end was near, and we were pretty much there; we just needed to have the conversation, and I was devastated. I was not surprised because when I thought about it, I would leave me too – I mean, ironically, I partially did when I transitioned. I felt integral admitting that what was happening was due to me; I totally owned that. However, I could no longer delude myself thinking I had anything left in me to give others what they needed. And as much as I can blame myself to try make others feel better and make things right, I was very aware I was running on fumes if anything at all. I was in no shape to save myself, and I'm not sure I even wanted to. As I came to the final realization that this was done, it truly became the saddest day of my life. That's really saying something as I reflect on the despair I experienced in my life to that point. Thirty-two years, gone. Puff. Done. Thinking back, it still brings tears to my eyes.

My only priority was our girls, and we both wanted what was best for them. I can honestly say that was my intention, however, I feel I'm too close to it all, and I cannot control someone else's perception. I remember being so upset and angry that I hurt people I loved, and, once again, a great sadness came over me. But after that evening, I realized that the best thing for her was, undoubtedly, to be away from me. I always wanted what was best for my family. I didn't care about what was best for me. I never did. Throughout my life, I did things I thought would make a difference in how I felt, but they never did. The only thing that made me feel better was spending time with my family. If they were happy, I felt happiness. So that was always my focus, and now that was gone.

I must acknowledge yet another reaction I had to all of this. As bizarre as it seems, when my wife told me she wanted to leave and it became apparent it was the best thing for her, I too felt a sense of relief.

I knew that my only path to survival was to transition,
but I was afraid to blow up my life, so I wasn't fully committed
to that plan.
My fear of how that would affect others was
the last thing holding me back.
They were more important than me.

I came to terms with everything else but not that. This was something that was going to take time. And with that, my decision to transition was pretty much locked in.

March 19, 2015

And, so it ends…

Not a good day, or night last night. My wife asked to speak to me when I got home from work at 8:30. At which point she announced that she is moving out, probably as of May 1, maybe sooner. She has contacted a divorce lawyer and wants a formal separation on the way to a divorce. A very quick conversation, about 20 minutes. I told her honestly where I was in my headspace. That I had been working with two specialists around all of this and that I don't have all the answers or know how it is going to end. I told her that there was nothing that she could call me, nothing that she could think of me, that I haven't said or thought already. Nobody hates this more than I do. I didn't choose this. Nobody hates the male me more than I do. No one can be more sad or depressed about this than I am. So, go ahead, rant at me. Get it out of your system. I have cried every day for the past six months. I can take it. And the conversation ended shortly thereafter… And that is that.

The remaining time together was spent quietly. Preparations were made for the separation and the move. I was totally expecting I would be the one asked to leave. But, she offered instead. It was a very gracious thing for her to do, and I am thankful to this day. She said I had enough going on in my life, and I needed some stability to deal with all the changes I was going through. It was kind of her.

Some days were better than others. I continued to make meals for both of us. I still took the dog for walks. It was... civil. There were days I was not able to keep it together with one Sunday, in particular, being quite bad. I recall being in the kitchen, making dinner as usual. I did most, if not all, the meal prep as it was something I quite enjoyed doing. But for some reason, I totally lost it and started crying uncontrollably. I didn't have the energy to contain my sadness anymore. I told her I was sorry, and that I was really trying, but I just wasn't having a very good day.

What I needed and wanted was to be hugged - from anybody actually. So, I sucked it up and finished getting dinner ready. Such are the trials and tribulations of people who deal with Gender Dysphoria. The result is the impact it has on their loved ones as it takes over your life. It ain't pretty, to say the very least. But, it was what I had to deal with, and so I did. Or at least I tried. There is no manual or playbook for this, so I was making it up as I went along. I know I could have done many things, if not everything, better. But, at the moment, all I had was what was in my head as scary as that was.

March 31, 2015

It is interesting the roller coaster we (those with GD) are all on. At least for me it is. Emotionally, I seem to be all over the place. One day the world is my oyster, the next, well not so much. Last night was one of those "not so much" instances. It is amazing where the brain goes sometimes when you leave it unattended. I was vacillating between feeling like a failure as a man and a husband, to feeling successful as a parent. Then, back to feeling like a failure as a man. How does one do that? Fail as a man I mean? All you have to do as a male is just show up. That is it. But I failed at that. I have no male attributes except physical ones, which, as one would imagine, I am not particularly enamored with. When I am around my wife, I am constantly reminded of both of those failures. And I feel bad. I mean really bad about that for her. I failed her. Something that I never wanted to do. But, the bottom line is that I have. Period. Full stop. She is still very bitter right now, but civil towards me, so we are doing okay, but I am sure she is looking forward to moving out next month and being away from me. So how did I fail as a man? I would guess that is because I am not a man? Duh!

And then, just when I thought things couldn't get worse, they did. I received a call on April 7th that my mom passed away. While I wasn't close to my mom - biggest understatement ever - I broke down and cried. I just didn't have the energy to deal with one more thing. I remember that my wife, who was in the room when I took the call, actually gave me a hug. I thank her for that. And then, off I went to deal with my family and the funeral.

To say this was a trying time is like saying Hurricane Katrina was a summer shower. I didn't have much time to prep or make arrangements, but I did. I flew halfway across the country to be with my brother and sister, and then we all made the five-hour drive to where my parents live for the funeral. Fortunately, most of the arrangements had been made. My parents had made all the decisions while they were alive, so for the most part, we just had to execute those plans. However, we did have to make specific decisions regarding the eulogy, like who would do readings and other rituals at the service. Much to the credit of my sister, my brother, and his wife, it all got done. My dad held up quite well. I, on the other hand, well… not so much.

Every day while there, I experienced massive triggers around my Gender Dysphoria. First and foremost, I did not tell anyone about the divorce. This would only have devastated them further. My family loved my wife, and with good reason, but this was not the time or the place. This was about my mom, not about me, so I didn't want to go there. Second, I was not going to tell my family I was transgendered. Again, not the time or place. So, I kept all of that suppressed, and that took a huge amount of energy. Then to top it all off, I had to wear a suit and dress shoes on more than one occasion, which just about put me right over the edge. I was pretty much a mess. Fortunately, I have a great deal of experience hiding it; people combating Gender Dysphoria are great actors. We try desperately to act how we're supposed to, how our families and society expects us to.

I make a great duck.
All is calm on the surface whilst paddling like hell
in a full panic underwater.

April 11, 2015

Made it through the funeral yesterday. Did find a few minutes of quiet time to say goodbye to my mom and tell her I was her other daughter. That felt good for me and gave me some peace. At many times throughout the day I didn't feel good. I have never felt so alone. Everyone had spouses to lean on. I did not. Sure, I had my brother and sister, but I was too busy being strong for them and for my father, attending to details, helping with arrangements, and making sure things got done.

But once it was all over, and I was alone in my bedroom, I had a total meltdown. I lost it. Major cry. I felt like I was grieving the loss of so many things all at once. My mom, my marriage, my wife, my male me. It was just all too much, so I lost it. But, finally managed to fall asleep.

It was now mid-April, and plans for the separation were in full swing. Once again, I was sad. I knew there was no point in delaying it, and yes, it was the best thing. I get that. The truth is that it still hurt. It didn't do much for my sense of self-esteem, particularly when I was feeling so vulnerable and didn't have any to begin with. Then, the day came. I was instructed not to be at the house that day for obvious reasons. So, I stayed away. But once again, I felt crappy. And, I get it. But still, it wasn't an easy pill to swallow.

This chapter in my life is particularly painful, and I feel the need to talk extensively about it. I think the biggest reason is that a lot of people in my community go through this. They go through it in silence without anyone knowing what they are enduring or the loss they are experiencing. Society must understand that these decisions we make regarding our lives and all we do to survive are not taken lightly. It's all very painful. We don't choose to hurt anyone, but at the same time, if we don't do something, we hurt ourselves - sometimes fatally. Unfortunately, it's not right, but it is the situation we face. That is a super frustrating part of all of this for me. It feels like people don't understand the pain or anything else about this.

Do they know Gender Dysphoria was at the root of all of this? Do they know what Gender Dysphoria can do to a person? Do they know that being transgender is not a choice? All of this makes me really, really sad, and frankly, a bit angry at the same time. People who choose not to educate themselves frustrate the hell out of me.

I know I'm not the only one who experienced excruciating pain. I do. I'm not that stupid. I know everyone in my family went through pain as a result of what I went through. Of course, I know that. There were many nights I was unable to sleep, knowing that I caused them pain. People living with Gender Dysphoria are caught in the quintessential catch 22. No matter what we do, someone will get hurt. And we live with this and like this, every day, stuck between a rock and a stupid place. I also acknowledge and accept that I caused my ex-wife's actions and reactions described here, and I don't blame her or hold any malice toward her.

My aim is not to put anyone in a bad light. My goal is to illustrate what individuals in my community go through with our families, to share why we deny who we are, and why we experience so much conflict. It is also to acknowledge what spouses and family members of a transgender person go through. Their feelings are legitimate and not uncommon. You are not alone. You have the right to own your feelings. But at the same time, my hope is that you also recognize that we are not willing participants. We do all of this because we have to, not because we want to.

It is important for family members to seek out support and to receive counsel or guidance from a therapist. I am relieved to say that, at least in this decade, there are more and more therapists who are trained and familiar with helping people who may find themselves in similar circumstances. Sometimes life sucks, and I find some consolation knowing that others out there do not have to be alone. There are now support groups forming for family members of someone who is transitioning to allow them to acknowledge and work through their feelings in their own time and not to feel bad about having them. It is important to take advantage of this knowledgeable support for everyone involved.

Truth

April 25, 2015

So, this is what trans people have to endure. No wonder we are terrified to come out and would rather suffer in silence !

This is another piece of my story I want to spend time on - the whole process of telling our two amazing daughters. This may be, in fact, the most painful and challenging part of my journey, and I don't think there is a good way to share this. It certainly didn't end up being the way it worked out for me, that's for sure. That would be the *opposite* of good! But it is what it is. I can apologize until the cows come home, but that won't do any good. I've already said, I'm *sorry*, a bazillion times. Again, it doesn't make it any better.

During the time all this occurred, our two girls lived in another city three hours away. They were working and living their lives. I hoped to tell them what was going on in small digestible bites - separation first; my Gender Dysphoria second. That's not what happened as it turns out. I ended up telling them about both the separation and my diagnosis with Gender Dysphoria on my own. There were many tears, so many tears. Of course, my girls were devastated. So was I. We sat there together and saw our whole life as a family dissolve in a matter of minutes. This really, really sucked.

I had no idea how to go about this, how to do this to the people I love, how to have this conversation in a way that wouldn't overwhelm everyone. I discovered that there isn't a *right* way to do this. I wanted to break the news down into two distinct chunks, the separation and the whole transgender thing. I wanted to give them time to breathe between the impact of each piece of news – to allow them the space to process one before moving on to the next. But, that was not to be because I was told what to do. It was insisted I tell them everything in one foul swoop. I recall thinking, *So, drink from a fire hose it is then,* and it was awful. I'm not going into more detail because it is still too painful, and it would not serve any purpose. There were instances of empathy and acceptance, along with total confusion and devastation. It broke my heart, and all I can say is that this was not my intention.

I felt total contempt for me on the part of my wife. This not only broke my heart, but it killed my spirit, and I felt like a total monster and completely worthless. I want to believe this was not her intention and that her response was motivated by her lack of awareness and understanding about how being diagnosed with Gender Dysphoria affected me. I believe it was a lack of knowledge all around that created this reaction to the entire situation. But, what I felt deep within me created my perception of her disdain for me, which then became my reality as a result of my emotional state during a time of confusion and mental fragility.

I recall feeling extremely small, insignificant, and alone. One saving grace was that one of my daughters wanted to spend some time with me immediately after the event to talk things through. This was very helpful as it gave us a chance to have a calm and rational conversation after the initial shock. I felt better after we talked, and I am thankful to her for providing me with a sense of not feeling so alone. I honour that my other daughter needed time, and I understand that is why her mother whisked her away immediately after the announcement. Everyone reacts differently and needs different things. I respected the need for each to deal with this in their own way, and I wanted to support them. Granted, I admit that I didn't always do that very well because I was also absorbed in the trauma we were all so desperately trying to manage. Within all our levels of awareness, I believe we each did the best we could at the time. I sometimes wonder if I would do things differently now, and maybe I would. But then, I remind myself that there is no right way to do this; it was just something we all needed to experience and learn from.

So, it was done and off I went to start my life on my own back home. It seemed like the longest three-hour drive of my life. My head was spinning and not in a good way. I relived every second of our conversation and visualized their reactions over and over again. I felt the hurt and confusion I caused, and it was such a crappy feeling. A bit of balance came when I experienced the immense warmth from my daughters' hugs before I left. This glimmer of hope is what kept me going for a very long time. My daughters made me aware that I needed to focus on the good, to look through the gigantic piles of awful and hang on to one thread of warmth and love. If I hadn't found that, I don't think I would have found any good within this.

I got home, physically tired of driving six hours in one day and emotionally exhausted from everything else. I was back with my pup, my only companion who met me wagging her tail and a smile on her face. She was always happy to see me, and trust me, that was not a familiar feeling, so I gratefully accepted the love. We settled in for the night and began the next chapter of our lives, leaning on each other for companionship. That is how this significant day ended, with her curled up beside me in bed in restful slumber. Oh, how I envied her.

What was next was telling my sister and brother. So, I made plans to tackle that.

May 20, 2015

It was quite a weekend. I flew to the east coast to visit with my brother and sister and their families. They all now know about my separation and transition. It couldn't have gone better! They were sad about the separation, but so very thrilled about my transition. Uber supportive! There were many tears, but tears of joy that I get to finally be happy and at peace with who I am. Also tears of sadness as they were so upset that I have denied being my real self for so long. My sister told me that she can't imagine how hard my life has been. She said that if someone told her she had to dress as a man the rest of her life, she would throw herself off the balcony. So, for me to have to dress and act as a man all my life when I am a woman, she doesn't know how I did it. She can't imagine the pain…

My brother (and his family) stepped up to the plate big time. Had a big celebration dinner to welcome Erin into the family. It was awesome. Both my brother and sister are very protective of me now. I recall vividly their proclamation "if someone has a problem with you, they are going to have a problem with us." So that is now everyone. My sister, her husband, their two kids (in their late 30s), my brother, his wife and their four kids (in the late 20s and 30s). All done. Moving on...

It was time to tell my family, my brother and sister. This was going to be a lot. But, it had to be done. I was afraid, but not as terrified as I was approaching the conversations with my ex and daughters. I knew in my heart that, one way or another, me and my siblings were all going to be fine. Maybe not right away or with both at the same time, but at some point overtime, everything was going to be okay. My main concern was to be able to tell them what was going on in my life without any of us feeling overwhelmed. Somehow, I needed to determine how to avoid information overload.

I already decided that the whole truth was the only way to go- the good, the bad, and the ugly of it all. I felt at peace with the fact that I was able to do this in a way that was comfortable for me and, especially, for my family, unlike the last time. I chose to have the conversation without throwing anyone under the proverbial bus, and that took a bit of thought; actually, quite a bit of thought. Once again, no manual to fall back on. Damn that. But, I finally formulated a plan that felt good, and I made the phone call.

I called my sister to see if it was okay to come down on the Victoria Day weekend, a three-day holiday in May in Canada. I figured it was going to take that long to get through it and leave time for damage control if necessary. I also knew they wouldn't think anything of me flying there for the long weekend because I had done that before. The difference this time was that I would be coming without, who they thought was still, my wife. Of course, my sister said it would be wonderful to have me down, and we finalized the plans. I sent her my flight itinerary, so she knew my exact arrival and departure times. She did note that I was coming down alone and clarified if it was just me coming. I replied it was. It was odd that she asked that, so I knew she suspected something. But there was no way I could have avoided that pre-visit stress.

I planned to arrive on Saturday morning and depart late Monday afternoon, giving us time to have lengthy conversations if required. And if not, then it would be a bonus to have more time with my siblings. I could have arrived on Friday night, but I knew she would want to get into it as soon as I arrived. In my mind, starting that conversation late Friday night would have ended in two possible outcomes. The first one was that we would be tired and not get through it all, which would leave a bunch of questions unanswered. In that scenario, I knew no one would get much sleep, and we would face the next day exhausted. The alternative was that she insisted we get through it all that night, and we would end up going into the early hours of the next morning. Going to bed at that time would result in the strong possibility of a sleepless night and waking up even more exhausted to start the next day. Either way was not a good plan.

Arriving first thing Saturday morning was the best possibility within a difficult situation. In hindsight, I do think it was the right thing to do. I headed to the airport and started this journey. Everything was on time, and my sister greeted me at the airport. It was an uneventful 30-minute ride to her place. I don't think either one of us wanted to open the can of worms, at least not just yet, not in the car. However, that was not longed-lived. When we arrived at her place, I greeted my brother-in-law, and before I even took my coat off, she looked at me and asked me what the hell was going on. There we were, the three of us huddled around the kitchen island with the time arriving for me to execute the communication strategy I came up with. Again, right or wrong, it was all I had, and I took a deep breath.

I have three pieces of news to discuss. One is very sad, one's okay, and the other, I don't know how it's going to go. And I started. The first piece was that my wife and I separated, and we're heading for divorce, which was sad. The second was that it was relatively amicable - okay, so that may have been a little white lie, but we weren't planning on taking advantage of each other. And last, well, that's when I went into my somewhat rehearsed story. The one about being diagnosed with Gender Dysphoria 17 years ago, but at the time deciding not to act upon it. The one about the dysphoria getting worse over time, that I was re-diagnosed, and it was confirmed. The one that means I'm transgender and will be starting the process to transition.

Well, that had to sink in. My sister said she knew something was up as soon as I told her I was coming alone. She thought I was going to tell her that I was gay. Still being attracted to women as a woman, I was gay, but that was a conversation for another time. While there was some shock, it was nothing catastrophic! But that was short-lived when I looked at my brother-in-law, who was in tears. Uh-oh. Now I've done it. I immediately apologized because I didn't mean to hurt anyone. He told me it wasn't that, but he was so sad I had to suffer so much for so long. I wasn't prepared for that, and it moved me so much.

*When he expressed so much understanding
and compassion for all of this,
my heart immediately told me I was going to be okay.*

For the next hour or so, we had a more detailed discussion that mostly comprised of me answering their questions. And they were great questions. I'm sure they felt some of them might have been a little too personal, but what about all of this isn't personal? I didn't want anything to be awkward, so I decided to lay down very simple ground rules: nothing was off the table, and I agreed to answer any and all questions. At the very least, I owed them that. And after all, I was learning not to be ashamed or embarrassed about any of it. It is the story of who I am. The only caveat I had was that they needed to keep one thing in mind - because I was willing to answer all questions, they needed to be careful what they asked! I told them, *If you don't want to know, don't ask.* That was more of a heads up because some answers may deal with certain parts of my anatomy, what was about to change and how, including the surgery I was going to undergo. The bottom line was that we had a very great first discussion, and I found that I could breathe again.

Next up were my brother and his family. This, for whatever reason, was not as much of a slam dunk for me. In my mind, to say my relationship with my brother was strained was probably quite accurate. It may just be my perception, but while we did get along, we were not that close. This was one of those cases whereby, although I just didn't feel I could accurately predict their immediate reaction, in the long run, I knew we were going to be okay. Regardless, I also knew it was going to take time.

My sister sent my brother a text asking if he and his wife were available for coffee and a chat sometime the next day.

The phone rang two minutes later, so that must have tweaked something on their radar. It was my brother suggesting we come over after dinner that day. Perfect. The sooner, the better as far as I was concerned. In some ways, I was anxious, but in others, not so much. I mean, when I think about it, nothing they could say was going to change my mind. I am who I am. The timing worked out perfectly because it allowed my sister and brother-in-law time to digest the information that was suddenly thrust upon them earlier that day. We had dinner, and they asked a few more questions before we headed off to my brother's house.

It was only a ten-minute drive, so, fortunately, there was little time to get anxious. After initial greetings, we headed into the living room, and I recall that all eyes moved towards me. I immediately began telling what became my *go-to* story. Given that the format I used with my sister was successful, I followed the identical style. *I have sad news, okay news, and not sure news.* It was about a ten-minute narrative, and then the questions began. My sister-in-law spoke first, stating that she was very sorry to learn we were getting divorced. So was I. That was right after I told them the *sad news.* Then I continued with the *okay news* and the *not sure news*, and the room became very quiet. After a few moments, my brother simply said, *Okaaay.* Shocked, I'm sure he was processing and trying to come up with an appropriate response.

What followed next was ninety minutes of questions and answers. Some of the questions were similar to those my sister asked, and some were very unique. My one niece was home visiting at the time and supplied additional information from her perspective, so that was very helpful. My sister commented that it was the second time she heard my story, and she learned more the second time around. I get that, because it's a lot to digest. It's like drinking from the proverbial firehose; a lot comes out at one time! There is the medical aspect of it, that this is a condition I was born with, and then the mental and emotional side of it. I am always reminded of the persistent and lengthy mental anguish that everyone in my community must endure. I know it takes time, and that is one thing I learned through all of this - I needed to give people plenty of time to work through it. For most, it was nowhere on their radar screen and a complete shock. They had a lot to process and had to figure out how all of this impacted me, as well as how it impacted them.

For many, learning what Gender Dysphoria is will be something new. For some, it will be the first time they ever heard the term, so dealing with the basics is an excellent place to start. For others who are more familiar with the term and condition, more detailed information is what will likely be asked for. They also need to know what it means to transition, the steps involved, the timelines, and the expectations. And that for many, fear is something that needs to be overcome. There are some genuine fears, like losing a job or a home. It's difficult to provide a plan for how one deals with all of this because every situation is different. Everyone's journey through transition is unique; there is no *one size fits all* scenario.

Patience and being able to roll with things plays a big role
when managing all the variables that can present
from one day to the next.
I had fifty-five years to digest this
so, I also didn't expect my family would be able
to process this overnight.

I had to learn to give myself and everyone around me the gift of time. I wasn't going to transition in isolation, and I was grateful there were, and still are, a lot of people on this roller coaster ride with me.

As we were getting ready to leave, my brother asked if we would like to come for dinner the following night. Perfect. That was quite a significant sign in my book. It told me that we were not only going to be alright, but we were already alright. It also provided them with some time to try to process all of this. I was sure they would have plenty of questions once they sat on it overnight. I was more than happy to come back for dinner, this time with more of their family present, and to continue the conversation at whatever level or pace they were ready for.

That left the following day for a bit of a breather with my sister. We chatted about many things, not just me, which was welcome. All this talk centred around me was somewhat exhausting. I was fine with it to a certain extent because it was what I had to do and what was needed, so I just went with it. I also realized just how physically exhausting it was. If I recall correctly, we all had to have a nap at one point! Eventually, it was time for us to head over to my brothers.

Upon arrival, I was completely overwhelmed, but in a good way! My brother and his family went way above and beyond the call of duty. They arranged a fantastic dinner party with flowers and pink decorations, including rosé sparkling wine. Good thing I like pink! And if that wasn't enough, my brother gave a very short, but heartfelt toast. It was, in his exact words, to welcome his sister, Erin, to the family. It was incredibly moving, and I was both surprised and touched. But that is my brother. He has this knack of not saying much, but when he does, it is virtually always on point. And he didn't disappoint this time! We continued to enjoy the evening and an excellent meal. There were more questions and discussions about what it meant to have Gender Dysphoria and be transgender. But the majority of the evening consisted of family chatter. It was perfect! A wonderful evening to remember.

On to the next day, which was the day I flew home. I still had to have one last conversation with my nephew, my sister's son. He is married and has children of his own and is the first-born grandchild, so I knew him the longest. He was also the only child my sister had who lived in the same city as her, so it was easy for him to come over. When he did, once again, I went through what had comfortably become my *Spiel*. His reaction was much as I expected, complete acceptance. He had a bunch of questions, and I answered them all. He tended to focus more on the physical aspects and wanted to know what was going to happen to me when I transitioned. It was good to go through this, not only for him but for my sister. Once again, she picked up on things the third time around that she hadn't the first or second time. Proof that this whole thing is a lot to digest.

So that was that. With my mission accomplished, all those closest to me and the most important in my life were told. And wonder of wonders, I still have most of them in my life. I know this is not the norm. I know many people in my community are disowned by members of their family, even their parents, and to me, that is just unfathomable! The truth is, I experienced that alienation with my de facto parents, and it was and still is soul-crushing. But, I just had to accept it and move on. Just like so many, I am basically the same person today. I don't know what drives these types of outcomes. I believe that a lot has to do with not understanding or even wanting to understand. Like every other medical condition, there is a lot to learn, and it is imperative to educate not only ourselves but everyone around us. Fortunately, the current climate has changed somewhat concerning a more elevated acceptance of the transgender community. There has been quite a bit of press in the recent past. Case in point is Caitlyn Jenner, and like her or not, she is impactful in putting my community in the spotlight. She started a national conversation that was decades overdue. I know from my experience, for those who are not quite sure what I am talking about, I simply mention her name and others completely tune in. That then allows me to take the conversation where I need it to go depending on my circumstances. So, I thank you, Caitlyn.

The only other sidebar to my weekend with my family was a comment made by my brother. He spoke to my sister-in-law the following day and mentioned that he knew all along that something wasn't right with me but couldn't put his finger on it. Welcome to my world! I was glad he was able to recognize that. And, while we weren't close in the past, I had a good feeling this was going to change for the better. I wasn't disappointed. I feel we are closer now. In fact, I am closer to everyone in that family, and that is a good thing!

May 18, 2015 – Email to my family...

Thank you to you all. You have no idea how much your acceptance, love, and support means to me. I realize that all of this around my journey was a surprise and/or shock. But your response was so overwhelming welcoming that I feel so very fortunate to have you all in my life.

It has been a long hard road for me at times in my life, but am looking forward to my future with excitement and with the knowledge I will finally be happy and that we will be there for each other. I will be fine. We will be fine.

I welcome any questions at any time and will keep you up to date with the results of various consultations and changes along the path to becoming who I am meant to be.

I return home light of heart, renewed in spirit, and strong in conviction.

With much love,

Your sister, Erin

Another area of life that I knew would be impacted by all of this was my neighbourhood. We were part of a small community of really lovely people in a very friendly area of the city. We lived there for over 24 years, and there were pretty much the same people still living on our street since we moved there. We watched each other's kids grow up, and we enjoy great gatherings for things like July 1st celebrations and weekend BBQs. We looked out for each other and lent a hand when required. I was hoping to stay in that neighbourhood if possible. While I wanted it to all be okay, I wasn't sure it would be. My mantra is to prepare for the worst and hope for the best. I was hopeful.

Given that I was now living full-time as my authentic self - except at work, that would follow - I knew it was time to have *the chat* with my neighbours, especially because I wanted to interact with them as Erin and not have to sneak around my own home. So, I decided to plan for that. I thought it would be easiest and best to tell each family independently. I believed this would accomplish two things; it would allow me to address individual questions in a manner tailored to their reactions, and it would give me the time I needed to answer all their questions in detail. I also knew I wanted to do this in a very compressed time frame. I didn't want the chance for any rumours to start with misinformation getting out. There were three key families I wanted to get to, so I set about creating a plan of attack.

Since the way I went about this with my family worked well, I decided to use the same approach, with a slight modification. They all knew we were separated because my ex took care of that on the day she moved out. Of course, everyone saw the moving van in the driveway, which opened the door for them to come over to see what was going on. She was kind enough only to share the basic information, which was that we were separating. She could have completely annihilated me, but she didn't. I am thankful to her for that. I selected the first family to tell and set up a time. I started my story off by telling them that I had a medical diagnosis 17 years ago, and then I launched into my monologue. Once again, it was about a 10 to 15 minute monologue on my part after which I opened the discussion up to questions. Each one of them expressed sadness at the pending divorce, but every one of them was accepting of my Gender Dysphoria and transitioning.

I told them all that I wanted and needed to be comfortable in my own home, my yard, and my neighbourhood, but if that wasn't possible, I would move. They assured me this wasn't a problem and asked what I needed from them and what they could do to help. The acceptance and compassion were nothing short of amazing. One down.

Beautifully, there were comical moments with some of the couples. One stated they had seen a new woman in my home and was sort of wondering what was going on. It turns out, that was me! One of the wives thought she was the only one in the neighbourhood talking about it. She was certain no one else was saying anything. That was when her husband chimed in that *oh, yes, there certainly was*. He informed both of us that all of the guys had been *checking me out*. That made me laugh out loud!! In the end, the conversation ended with a big hug from both of them.

The next one didn't quite go as planned in that it took a bit longer to set up than I wanted. I was hoping to catch her when she was home, but because she worked full-time and shuttled two kids to numerous activities, she didn't have much free time to socialize. So, I decided to try a different approach. I decided to do a *fly- by* her office to see if I could catch her there because she worked for the same organization I did. Due to the fact it was at work, we didn't have as much time as I would have liked. But I used the same approach, which, once again, seemed to work. She had a few questions, and although shocked liked everyone else, she was accepting and supportive. I mentioned to her that I already told the other neighbours in our circle, so she was free to speak with them about it. I knew she was quite close to them and wanted her to know it was okay for her to chat with them if she needed or wanted to. Two down.

When I got home that night, I called the couple I told earlier to let them know I had a chat with her and encouraged her to call them. They replied she already had as soon as she got home that afternoon from work. They said she was quite upset. Crap! I was hoping this wasn't going to happen. I asked if they thought it would be a good idea if I spoke with her again to discover what she was upset about and hopefully not lose a friend. What they told me next was not what I expected.

They said, *Oh no, it wasn't that she was upset with you, but that she was upset with herself.* Apparently, for the previous three weeks or so, she was throwing me – male me- under the bus big time. She was upset because she noticed a strange woman in my house, driving my cars, and looking quite comfortable in the setting. She immediately surmised that I must have been having an affair while still with my wife because I couldn't possibly be in a new relationship that quickly after my separation. She was not amused with me, to say the least. Then, upon learning what was really going on, she was super upset with herself for thinking something like that about me! Well, of course, on the one hand, it was quite comical. And I, being someone with no class, had to laugh out loud. On the other hand, it was somewhat validating for me.

The fact that people could actually believe I was a woman was quite surprising, particularly at this early stage of my transition.
To this day, we are still good friends.

That left one more couple I wanted to share my circumstances with. I admit, out of the three neighbours, this couple was the one I was the most nervous about. They were nice people and great friends. What I wasn't sure about was how accepting they were of the LGBTQ community, or if they were even familiar with all the different variations within the sexual and gender continuum. I wanted them to be the last ones so that I could judge my chances for success. Given the other two conversations went well, I was more confident going into this one. I managed to arrange some time to speak with them later on a Sunday morning a few days later.

The time came, and off I went next door. I had no idea how this was going to turn out, but I went into their home with a smile and mock confidence. After initial pleasantries, I moved through my story with the usual timeframe, and then stopped and waited for questions. He got it immediately, knowing what Gender Dysphoria is. She did not know what I was talking about. So, at that moment, I decided to try something different.

I asked if she knew who Caitlyn Jenner was. She said she did. I told her that was me and she immediately got it. Okay, now we're all on the same page. Just as I had told the others, I let them know that all I wanted to do was live my life, do my job, and continue to contribute to our community, but if I felt that wasn't going to be possible, I would most certainly consider the option of moving. The reaction of both of them, though different, was beautiful. She asked, *Is that all?* She was afraid I was going to tell them I was going to be putting the house up for sale! She was totally fine with me and my news. He said there was nothing in their house for me but love. I started to cry. It was such a simple yet powerful emotion. It reminded me of how fortunate I was to have such good people in my life.

That was it - done. The rest of the neighbours could find out on their own from these folks. I didn't have the time or energy to go to every house. And in the end, that worked out well. At the next block party, I was welcomed by everyone and was the recipient of some great hugs. All of this reiterated that there are still good, decent, loving people out there. I understand why we, as a trans community, are terrified about coming out. I have lived it, and it is sad to say that my experience with sharing who I am is not the norm. Many are disowned by family and alienated by their community. I realize that I can never be sure about what my life is going to be like. The only thing I know is that, no matter what that looks and feels like, it will always be better than the alternative.

It was at this time that I realized there was still a lot of hard work to be done.

Conviction

May 25, 2015

Had a session earlier in the week with my long time therapist about how my weekend went with my family. It was still emotional for me to recount. She was totally blown away by my family's response and even she was overwhelmed and had tears. So, there we were, both crying. But she said that after all the tears after all the years that I have had in her office, it was about time we had tears of joy! She gave me a big hug and was so very happy for me.

It was now time for some really hard work to begin. I scheduled a meeting with my gender therapist who I recently added to my medical team. I figured I would have a lot to work through and talk about immediately following my visit with my brother and sister, and I wasn't wrong. We had an intense session, to say the least. Not intense with respect to conflict between us, but intense in that I was trying to process a ton of emotion. Fortunately for me, she was able to get me back on track. She's been working with transgender people for over a decade, pretty much exclusively. I was not her first case by a long shot. She told me that during recent sessions with me while trying to figure this all out, to figure me out, she discovered I was a textbook case.

When we reviewed the narrative, that was my life, all the signs and typical markers were there. It was clear to her that I indeed suffer from Gender Dysphoria and was transgender. As such, it was time to start aligning with my correct gender, externally, and as my authentic self. I had so many *triggers* for my dysphoria that it was time. It was my time. So, together, we worked on a plan to prepare me for the rest of my life - my true life. No longer to be the shadow of who I really am. But to step into the light and the sunshine, to grow as a person and be true to me. And so, it began.

The first step was to get my biochemistry sorted out. For that, I needed to see an endocrinologist. Fortunately, there were two in the city of Ottawa who were accepting new transgender patients. She referred me to one of them to have my blood work and hormone levels checked. It was a two-hour drive from my home, but I didn't care. I had to get this done. That appointment was scheduled for about a month later.

The second thing she wanted me to do was to begin the transition to my true self. Now that I was living alone, and I was out to my family, it was time to start to experience living as, well, me. Mainly because it was time, and it would reduce if not eliminate virtually all of my triggers for anxiety attacks, depression, and other harmful aspects. It was also a requirement for any surgeries I might contemplate in the future. Physicians and surgeons who specialize in treating transgender people typically require that you live full-time in your correct gender for at least one year before even considering you as a candidate for surgery. That is to say, living 24/7 in your correct gender, out to everyone in your life, including family, friends, and employers. So that was to begin immediately. Right. No problem!

Actually, *Houston, we have a problem*! I wasn't ready to come out at work, not by a long shot. I wanted at least another year for that. While my therapist was a bit surprised by that, she understood my reasons. Essentially, I wanted time for the medical protocol to work its magic. I also wanted to make it super easy for as many people as possible to accept me as Erin. I didn't want to be seen as a *dude in a dress*. I knew the hormones would impact me not only mentally but physically as well. My body would be the beneficiary of sculpting, naturally created by the treatment. So, we made the decision that I would be *full-time* everywhere except for work. This is, oddly enough, a pretty common pathway, mostly because we live in fear of losing our jobs. It also encompasses having a fear of being the focus of ridicule, rejection and harassment. No one wants that, so we agreed our decision was the best thing for me. The critical point here is that it was the best thing for me. I am by no means stating this is the correct way to do it. I'm not sure there is a correct way. All I knew is that this was my way, and it was the best plan for me. Frankly, that is all that mattered at the time.

So, where to begin? I mean, don't get me wrong, I was super happy and excited that I was finally going to live congruently between gender and my identity. But on the other hand, I was a bit terrified; I won't lie. The first thing I decided to do was to assemble a medical team to oversee my treatments. While my family doctor was on board with respect to working with me and accepting who I am and my transition, he was not well-read in how to support someone who is transitioning medically. He wanted me to get an endocrinologist on board so that he had a specialist to contact. No problem, we had that covered, so I told him I was seeing one in less than a month, which he was pleased to hear. So, my team was just about complete. I had my family doctor, an endocrinologist, my regular therapist, and my gender therapist, all talking with one another to ensure I was in good shape, mentally, emotionally, and physically. There was one other person that I wanted on board, my athletic therapist.

I worked with her for a few years on a minor diving injury to my shoulder, as well as, the impact of stress on my neck and shoulders. I wanted her to know that I was going to undergo some changes to my body. I also wanted to share the source of my stress, which impacted my treatments with her. So, that week, at my regular appointment, I finally summoned up the courage to tell her. This is something that most people out in the *cisgender* world, which is a person whose gender is congruent with their sex assigned at birth, don't understand or appreciate. Every time we *out* ourselves, we open ourselves up to ridicule and rejection. And unfortunately, it happens more often than not in my community. But I was pretty sure I was on safe ground with her, and I wasn't wrong.

I explained my medical diagnosis of Gender Dysphoria and what my plans to now transition meant for me. She was so very sad to learn about my suffering and was thrilled that I was going now be able to become who I was meant to be - Me. She went through a list of things the medical protocol impacted. She also addressed the muscles and systems that would be affected, and she needed to pay special attention to.

She wanted to provide me with the best level of care to reduce any side effects to the best of her ability. This was all amazing, simply amazing! It was so much more than I could have hoped for.

She also had an expansive practice, with several staff and other specialists working for her, as well as a huge client base. I told her I did not want to impact her practice in any way or have her clients feel uncomfortable around me. I shared that I was still presenting as *male me* at work, and I would be presenting as such at my appointments because they were during working hours. I didn't anticipate any issues for her clients. Fortunately, she understood my approach and plan. As for me being transgender and the possibility of upsetting her employees, her response was quite simple - if it bothers any of them, they are not the kind of person she wanted working for her anyway. *Not your problem*, she said. Holy! To have someone support me so absolutely was fantastic. I can't thank her enough.

The next items on the list had to do with physical appearance, and that was quite the list. I knew the protocol would take care of most of them over time, but I needed a plan to deal with the here and now. It was time to figure that out. First up was hair. I was starting to grow my hair out and needed guidance as to how to make it work. I began the search for options on the internet, focusing on services available in my area. I felt I had a winner, or so I hoped, and I took the time to contact them.

The service I located works with women who have undergone cancer treatments, so very familiar with the challenges and the fragile nature of their clients. I called and asked to speak with the owner. I had a strategy in mind, and I wanted to be upfront with them.

I'm not ashamed of who I am, and if they couldn't deal with it,
I wanted to know that from the onset.

When I spoke with her, I told her I was transgender and that I wanted to discuss the possibility of using her services, but if she was uncomfortable with that, to let me know, no harm, no foul. Her response was priceless! *Oh sweetie, you're not my first rodeo, get your butt in here! No problem, of course, I am comfortable with that. It is who you are, and we are here to help. We have experience with other transgender clients, so don't worry about that anymore.* So, I immediately got my butt in there!!

To say that she and her staff were welcoming was an understatement. Oh, my gosh, she had a fantastic facility. She took me into a private styling room where she analyzed my hair pattern, and then proposed potential solutions, of which there were many. She and her staff support many women in different phases of treatment with different impacts. So, over the years, she developed a variety of solutions to address what works best for each. I was no exception to that consideration. In the end, we worked up a solution customized to my condition.

Next was how to deal with facial hair. While laser worked on my dark hair, grey hair is unfortunately immune to that technology. So, that meant I had to turn to electrolysis. Off I went in search of that service in my city. Once again, there was an option. I contacted the owner of the clinic and presented my scenario in much the same way I did to my hairstylist. I mean, hey, that seemed to work the first time, so why not try it again. I told her who I was upfront, stating once more that if she wasn't comfortable, please let me know now. The response was identical. I wasn't her first trans client, so we set up an initial consult. That turned out to be very successful. She agreed that electrolysis was necessary for the grey, but to continue with the laser treatments for my dark hair. Overall, that would make the process a bit more efficient. However, it was still going to take two years to remove all the hair from my face and neck. Having heard stories from other transwomen, I understood this going into the consultation, but it still sucked hearing it. I didn't have a choice. None. So, we set up a treatment schedule, and it began.

The next thing on my list was makeup, partly because it was still a bit of a necessity to conceal a bit of shadow from remaining dark facial hair. I also, just like the notion of wearing makeup. I know there will be those who get all riled up and start yelling at the page that not all women wear makeup! There is the opinion that I'm doing it just to pretend I am a woman and that society forces women to wear makeup. I need everyone to just calm down! This is a multi-billion dollar industry, and I'm pretty sure that it isn't just transwomen who buy and wear makeup. And yes, it might be a false social construct that women have to wear makeup to feel good about themselves. I, personally, know a TON of really brilliant, confident women who wear makeup because, well, they just like to! And that's me, so enough already!! It's time to move on.

Not knowing a lot about the subject, I decided to go to the experts. I took the bull by the horns and called my local Sephora store and booked a makeover. Once again, I told them who I was and a bit of my story. They were super receptive. They arranged an appointment with one of their makeup artists, who turned about to be the floor manager, so I was all set. To say I was nervous on the day of the appointment is a huge understatement! However, to give me some credit, I did book a time when I thought the store was not going to be too busy. Fortunately, I was correct. And that's a good thing because, like most cosmetics services, they do their makeovers in plain sight of the public.

Well, my esthetician couldn't have been more wonderful, and I had a super relaxing makeover! Needless to say, I learned a ton, and I also realized that I clean up pretty good. She said exactly what I was thinking, *You know what? You're going to be okay!* It was an affirming experience for sure. And again, it was something that reduced a trigger for me because I no longer had to look at that stupid male face, or at least, not as much. Fortunately, the changes from Hormone Replacement Treatment, eventually, took care of that permanently. The thing I wondered about then, and frankly, still wonder to this day is why every woman doesn't do this. I've seen so many major makeup disasters that could quickly turn around into something incredible. Maybe it's just me, but why do women think that they are born with a makeup gene, reluctant to work with an expert? Anyway, the bottom line is that working with this esthetician helped me prepare, and we are great friends to this day.

Over the years, I created meaningful relationships with all these people who willingly helped and supported me. They treat me like a valued person and see me for the woman I am. It is so wonderful to have services like this available. And yet, It saddens me that this is not always the case for people in the trans community. Some wonder why this is such a trying journey. I have been so fortunate, and try to remain hopeful that one day, it will be like this for everyone, regardless of gender, gender identity, sexual orientation, religion, ethnicity, or colour. Someday.

It was now time to find some support for my transition in the community; I was feeling the need to find my tribe. So, I did what everyone else has probably done at one point, and I asked Ms. Google. Fortunately, I found a link to a support group in my city established by two couples, one whose child transitioned to reflect their authentic self, and another couple whose husband transitioned. The group was very informal, meeting one Saturday every month. They were very welcoming to the *community* and encouraged anyone who was either transgender or had a family or friend who was transgender to attend the meetings. This meant there was always quite a mix of people present with those who were transgender at various stages in the transition process, some pretty much done, while others were mid-way, and still, others who hadn't started and weren't sure what to do or how to go about it. There were also family members who attended supporting someone in their lives who was transgender. At any given meeting, there were spouses, siblings, children, grandchildren, and grandparents who attended, and it was an incredible mix of people providing a great diversity of experience and thought.

Still, even with all that knowledge, I wasn't sure if this was the right group for me, whether it would meet my needs or if I would fit in. I decided to meet with someone from the group to have a chat about all of that. We talked for well over an hour and shared our stories. She encouraged me to share my insecurities and fears about all of this, and she was so very kind and generous with her time and thoughts. I owe her a great deal. She and her wife are both dear friends to this day.

I recall being somewhat overwhelmed at the first meeting because I was the new kid on the block. While everyone was very welcoming, it took me a while to feel at ease. This was mostly due to my own insecurities, and over time, I found it extremely comforting to be with all these people.

To have a sense of belonging to a community was something I desperately wanted, and quite frankly, needed.

When people are first diagnosed with Gender dysphoria and realize they are transgender, a common thing they experience is severe isolation. I was no different because, although I knew it wasn't true, in my heart, I felt that I was the only trans person in my city. Until one starts to make connections and develop a network, it can be very lonely.

But, feeling alone was not a foreign feeling to me at all. My entire life, I never felt like I fit in. I never really belonged to any community. My sense of identity was pretty much nonexistent, and it's hard to fit in when you don't know who you are or where you belong. It's sort of like being on the island of Misfit Toys, except you are still alone. There are no other toys there to relate to, and it's even more frustrating when everyone else around you has figured it out. That just reiterates your thoughts of being the odd person out, literally and figuratively speaking. So, this support group was somewhat of a lifeline for me. Everyone needs to feel they belong, and I believe we can all be that person for those searching for a *tribe*.

There was something else I wanted assistance with, and that was my look. Not in the physical sense per se, but the aesthetic. I didn't grow up learning about fashion as other girls did. What I did know is that I had no idea what looks good on me, or what my style is. So, once again, I decided to find help, to find someone who was an expert in personalized fashion. Fortunately for me, one of the foremost personal fashion consultants lived in my city, and I decided to reach out to her using my usual upfront approach. Luckily, it turned out not to be an issue because, even though she had little experience working with people in the trans community, she was extremely supportive and excited about the opportunity. We set up a time to meet to begin the process of creating my fashion profile. I admit I started getting excited as well!

When the time came, I went to her office and let her work her magic. She took about 20 different measurements, getting a really good idea of my body type. Then, she draped me in numerous yards of fabric to get a sense of colours that worked with my skin tone and physical features. In the end, it was a fantastic experience resulting in a portfolio of fabric colours being my palette to rely on when choosing clothing. In addition, she provided access to a personalized style profile via a computer program outlining every style detail accentuating my body - things like dresses, skirts, and including details like sleeve lengths, collar styles, shorts, long pants, waist styles, belts, shoes, jewelry, watches, glasses, bathing suits, and more. Literally, every aspect of clothing design was included to provide me with the perfect guide to buying flattering clothes.

This may sound a bit extreme, but in my mind, it was necessary. It was important for me to get this right. I was well aware of the many eyes that would be upon me once I came out, especially working in such a large organization with thousands of employees. I knew there were other transgender people out there waiting to come out, and some would be watching to see what the reaction to mine was. I wanted to provide them with a positive outcome, to show them they would be alright, and they would be supported. I didn't want to screw this up. You only get one chance to make a first impression, and I wanted to ensure I had the best chance possible to get it right. I also wanted to do whatever I could to make it easy for my colleagues when the time came for them to see me for who I am - a woman. It turns out, it was a very good thing to do. I can't thank my fashion consultant enough, and the additional benefit was that I created another friend and ally.

During this time, regular life activities needed to be maintained. One such event was taking care of my pup. Well, she was not a pup anymore, but a lovely 14-year-old yellow Labrador retriever, who I thought was extremely ill and I would have to make the tough decision to put her to sleep. It turned out she was just incredibly stressed out. She saw a lot of furniture and other items go out of the house when my ex-wife moved out, and she was left alone until I was allowed back into the house. I suspect she wasn't sure if anyone was coming back for her. She didn't eat for two days, which is pretty much unheard of for a healthy Lab and is certainly cause for extreme concern. After receiving advice from a few vets, I hand-fed her to get her eating again. I also spent as much time as I could outside with her and inside, comforting her by rubbing her while she lay at my feet. The vet prescribed anti-anxiety medication, which helped her to calm down after a few days. I thought I might sneak a few of them for myself - proof that a sense of humour is definitely something I needed to get through this. I believe happiness is the freedom to live my life out loud no matter what, and that's all I wanted. I just wanted to be happy.

May 13, 2015

Sometimes, just sometimes, it is good to really listen to yourself when you talk out loud to, well, really, no one. Case in point, my dog who is a little stressed out with all that is going on. Being alone with my pup, I try to calm her by speaking to her, just so she knows she is not alone in the house. So yesterday I found myself talking to her to calm her down when I said 'We are going to be okay. We can be alone without being lonely.' Well, that made me stop in my tracks. Maybe it is time I listen to my own advice?

Next, I had an appointment with an endocrinologist to

discuss the possibility of going on Hormone Replacement Therapy (HRT). Unfortunately, she was in Ottawa, a two-hour drive from my home, but hey, ya gotta do what ya gotta do, so off I went. I was somewhat nervous, not knowing what to expect. However, it turns out, there was no need because she was so competent. She sees a ton of trans people and is an expert in the area of HRT, having made this a significant part of her practice. She was super nice and immediately put me at ease.

She started by letting me know that my gender therapist who referred me to her, sent her my assessment, and I was approved to begin HRT. This approval was made after several appointments, including a review of my history. There was no doubt in her mind this was something I needed to do in order to begin the transition process. I was greatly relieved! The one thing about this entire process is that there are several *gatekeepers* one has to go through before beginning the transition process. While it can be frustrating, I do understand it. They want to make sure this is the correct path for their patient and that they are, in fact suffering from Gender Dysphoria and a suitable candidate for transition. They want to be sure they are ready within all areas of their well-being - mentally, emotionally, physically, and socially. This is a huge step, and many aspects are not reversible. So, it is imperative to be very sure.

May 7, 2015

I am getting nervous about starting HRT. Managing the process, keeping tabs on bloodwork, side effects and changes both physically and mentally. However, if I think about not going on HRT, I am scared of what would happen, not getting to be my true self would be catastrophic.

After a lengthy chat and review of my history with the endocrinologist, she concurred and laid out a plan of what HRT entailed to make sure I fully understood and was ready for it. Of course, I was ready for it. I had been ready for it my whole life. I just didn't realize it until 19 years ago. But now, I was absolutely ready to begin the next chapter of my life. So, she wrote my prescription for testosterone blockers and told me what to expect regarding the impact and side effects. Essentially, what these blockers do is inhibit the absorption of testosterone into my system. While I still manufacture it, it has nowhere to go, except out of my system. The side effect is that it is a *potassium-sparing diuretic*. This means that it causes the elimination of water and certain electrolytes such as salt and leaves behind potassium, another electrolyte. The solution is that I need to reduce the intake of potassium as much as possible and keep salt in my diet to manage the imbalance of my electrolytes,. That is easy for me because I crave salt; I always have. If there is an imbalance, it can cause muscle spasms, particularly in leg muscles, so I watched out for that. Typically, it means that I am not drinking enough water. I have to drink a ton of water every day, at least two litres.

She told me that she wanted to see me in three months and would look at my bloodwork then to see where I was, and we would go from there. If it was good, that is to say, if my testosterone levels were down, she would start me on estrogen to bring my levels up to normal. At my age, she didn't want me to take large doses of estrogen, but rather, the smallest dosage to get the required results. The thing with testosterone is that it is nasty stuff. It is much more powerful than estrogen, and if you have a lot of testosterone in your body, it will beat the crap out of estrogen. The goal was to reduce my T levels to almost zero, so it wouldn't take as much estrogen to do the job. Armed with that information and a prescription for T blockers, it was a relief to know that I was finally on my way! This was a happy day; a very happy day!!

Right from the beginning, the impact of HRT therapy was terrific! I didn't experience a physical effect right away, but I was surprised at how quickly I noticed an immediate impact mentally. Within the first week of being on T blockers, my brain seemed to calm down, and I was less agitated. The fog began to lift, and I found my ability to concentrate was stronger. I guess I found I was just a bit more at peace overall, and the quiet in my brain no longer took me down a rabbit hole to a darker place. The impact that hormones had on my mental and emotional well-being is quite incredible. It made me realize how much I was a victim of testosterone poisoning. For me, It is evil - pure evil. And now, it was on its way out the door. It was a long time coming, and so very much welcomed.

May 10, 2015

Had one of those WTF moments again last night. I was home having just returned from walking the dog. That is when I start to think, 'what am I doing?'. Rabbit hole. But I continue on and head to the kitchen to start dinner. While dinner is in the oven, I am sitting on the couch, looking out the bay window to the world, have a glass of wine in my hand and reading a magazine while music plays in the background. I catch my reflection in the mirror and that is when it hits me. This is why I am doing this. To live my life simply as me. Just little ol' me. And you know what? I like little ol' me.

Despite this, Gender Dysphoria is a formidable foe.
It will not go quietly into the night.

It fights back every inch of the way. It doesn't want to let go. Ever. It found a very comfortable home in my head for decades and wasn't about to cede any territory. While I had transitioned socially at this point for the most part, I had not with some in my life or at work. So, there were still moments.

June 8, 2015

Another WTF moment that was in the other direction. Just want this to be done. It is getting harder and harder to present as male and getting more uncomfortable for me with each passing day.

It was still a challenge at work with anxiety attacks hitting me at random and still needing to manage them. But I admit, they were not nearly as bad as before because the T blockers helped. It became clear to me that it was almost time to have the first conversation with my boss about suffering from Gender Dysphoria, being transgender, and planning to transition. Deep breath.

Resilience

June 11, 2015

Had the chat with my boss yesterday. It went extremely well!!
She is totally on board with my transition. We chatted for over 90
minutes. She had some questions and was sorry that I have been
unhappy for so long and that I hid it so well at work. She said that
I am strong enough to do this and that I have cultivated a lot of
political and personal goodwill in the organization and that she
doesn't anticipate any issues. And if there are, I have her complete
support as well as that of the office and overall department in
dealing with them quickly. I am so lucky to be working in such an
accepting organization.

And so, it began. This was the first step in the whole process of coming out at work. It was a significant one before the final act towards becoming my authentic self. And definitely became a process!! I knew it wasn't going to happen overnight, and quite honestly, I didn't want it to happen overnight. I wanted to make sure it was handled in such a way that allowed time for people to adjust. It was important they felt comfortable asking questions and that critical conversations were encouraged with department leadership. I wanted an educational component included in these dialogues.

Accurate knowledge was key for people understanding what I was about to do. I wanted to start the process with a very small group of key individuals and then work out from that core in concentric circles to, eventually, include the 300 or so people I worked with. It may seem like an extended timeframe to get this done, but this is what I thought would work for me. While I was in control of the timing, there were several factors I had to consider. The most important of which was my family at the time. This represented the final step in revealing Erin to the world as I started the rest of my life in totality as me.

The other factor was that it was becoming harder and harder to present as male me at work. In all other aspects of my life, I was Erin. But not at work. My brain started having real struggles with this. Even though I knew there was not only a light at the end of the tunnel, I also knew exactly how long the tunnel was and where it came out; that light was a long way off, and I was still battling bouts of dysphoria. It got to a point when I couldn't delay it any longer without consequences; bad consequences. I imagined there would be some who struggled with my decision or consider it a lifestyle choice. Nope, not a choice. It never was.

June 14, 2015

Having time to do some thinking last evening (which is never a good thing), my mind wandered to how to deal with the few who don't understand what I am doing and/or why. My question to them is If I can't be who I am, who am I supposed to be?

The next step was to go up the chain of command. That was the person leading our entire department. Once again, I was pretty sure the reaction would be supportive. But, my training over the years has taught me to mitigate the risk out of any situation, and I never like to take things for granted. I like to anticipate where the speed bumps or potholes might be and plan a detour to avoid them. So, in my mind, I constantly checked the route I took to figure out where issues might be and then prepared for them. The entire time, I heard *recalculating* in my mind. What if the environment ended up being unsupportive? What if there were issues serious enough that I lost my employment?

Layer this anxiety on top of the additional bonus of the dysphoria still kicking around, and things took their toll on my health again.

July 28, 2015

My monthly visit to my athletic therapists today turned out to be more about providing relief to my soul than my body. She only wants to see Erin from now on, no more male me. She said the stress of not being Erin is wreaking havoc on my system. So, the best thing for me to reduce that stress is to be me. My authentic self.

This was further confirmation that I needed to move

my plan forward and start the final step. One of the first conversations I had was with our Human Rights Office to get a sense of what legal standing I had, if any. It turns out that I not only had corporate policy on my side, but I had provincial legislation as well. That made me feel a bit more secure, but again, I never take anything for granted. So, I formulated a plan B for employment, just in case something went sideways. That became an ongoing exercise throughout the next year. It was, fortunately, one which I did not have to rely upon. I had a really good sense of that once I had the next conversation.

August 10, 2015

Well…another baby step today. Had "the chat" with the ultimate boss, the person who my boss reports to, the same person I report to directly on occasion for particular briefings. 90 minutes later, it was all good. Sorry, I am just getting teary eyed as I type this and recalling the conversation. Note to self, buy some waterproof mascara!

I started by describing my diagnosis, and sort of how I got to where I am now. I should mention that my direct boss was kind enough to join me, and I was very glad she was there to support me.

> **When I concluded my little story**
> **- that spiel of how I got to where I am -**
> **he simply asked, "How can I help?"**

And the conversation went on from there. He asked some very pointed questions like, how I am coping and what he and others in my department can do to support me. He suggested working from the comfort of my home as Erin on days I was not doing well and when the dysphoria spiked. I did not expect any of this, and it was very gracious of him to offer that possibility. We also talked about how communication to key personnel would be handled, as well as, to the masses when the time came. He had some brilliant insights concerning getting champions on board before any general announcement went out, and who he thought those people would be. So, in the end, it was an incredibly supportive conversation, and he was so kind, respectful, and caring. I couldn't ask for anything more from an employer and friend.

He also told me that someone else who worked for him at another organization transitioned just before he started there as the head. So, he was able to offer some examples of what worked well during that time. At the end of our chat, he offered to put me in touch with her so she and I could discuss how her transition went and how she managed it within her organization. His parting words to me were that my job was simply to do my job. And his job was to deal with any resistance or lack of acceptance or discriminatory behavior from anyone in the organization. He assured me that none of that was my responsibility, it was his. He took that very seriously.

December 29, 2015

I spent some time thinking about all of this, how everyone has reacted, family, friends, and now co-workers. And so far, I had not lost any friends. But what I have noticed is that over the past few months, I have made new ones. I have come to the conclusion that the number of friends you can lose is finite, but the number of new friends you can make is infinite. So, with that thought, I move forward every day.

This is all to say that the outcome, though not totally unexpected was above and beyond what I could have hoped for. I am so grateful for the supportive people in my life - another small victory and one more step towards the end of the tunnel to my new and true life. Everything was going so well. And then, all the wheels came off.

November 15, 2015

Off to the ER in the wee hours after experiencing a lot of chest pain. Living alone, I am paranoid about my health right now. Hours later, after a few tests, it appears to be a combo of indigestion, stress, and exhaustion.

As it turns out, this was not quite the correct diagnosis, but I do understand how they came to that conclusion. I had no other symptoms or any type of a heart-related issue. I didn't experience arm pain or tingling, headache, nausea, or any other typical symptoms. The discomfort only occurred when I lay down. I was in reasonable shape, so I had no predisposing factors either; I wasn't overweight or diabetic, and I didn't have high blood pressure.

Just to be on the safe side, they arranged a stress test for me, which I did a few weeks later. The result? Inconclusive. They had my heart rate up to 180 beats per minute, and I felt okay, but the monitor showed there might be something not quite right. Though they did tell me that told once the machine gets that high, it sometimes throws a false positive. So, I was off to another stress test.

That one had the same outcome. It was inconclusive, with another potential false positive. My cardiologist was pretty sure nothing was wrong and even advised that I could continue to run. At this point, I was doing five kilometres about three times a week. But once again, just to be on the safe side, he ordered another test. They wanted me to go for an angiogram, scheduled for early in the new year, which he felt would be much more accurate. All the while, I had this potential health issue looming in the back of my mind.

In the meantime, I continued to experience anxious moments, usually at night. They had been going on for several months. The mind is an amazing thing, and sometimes it can be a pain in the butt.

October 6, 2015

Well, one of those days. In quiet times at night, my mind sometimes likes to take a walk without a flashlight and sit in the dark. No clue why, it just does.

Lying in bed, it's quiet, and I became hyper-sensitive regarding any changes in my body, aches and pains, or any type of discomfort. Several weeks later, once again, at three o'clock in the morning, I experienced chest pains, and I panicked, heading off to the emergency room. The only bonus about having chest pain is that they see you right away. I had more tests, and there were no signs of a heart issue. However, I was still having chest pain, so they administered a nitroglycerin spray under my tongue. Low and behold, besides giving me a pounding headache, which is apparently a very common side effect, it did reduce my discomfort. Well, that got a bit of a reaction.

They agreed an angiogram was definitely a good idea, but if I was admitted, I wouldn't have to wait for the one I already had booked a few weeks away. So, that is what they did. It all happened with very little warning, and I found myself in a hospital room, waiting for another test. I was so fortunate that my youngest daughter, who was now back in our city, was there with me every step of the way. It was so amazing to have her with me. She reduced my fear and anxiety significantly, and I'm so lucky and thankful she was able to be there for me. My oldest daughter came home from Toronto as soon as she could, and I'm so grateful they could both be with me.

While lying in my hospital bed waiting for the test, which still took a few days, I had a visit from one of the resident cardiologists. This turned out to be a critical conversation. He began by stating that he read my medical file and reviewed my medications and knew I was in the process of transitioning. His question for me was, *How do you want to handle this? What can we do?* To say I was somewhat taken aback is a gross understatement. He asked about how to address me, what name and pronouns they should use. My initial reaction, given I was presenting as male coming in from the ER at three o'clock the previous morning, was to use my male name and male pronouns. My thought was that it would be easier on the staff. Then a little voice in my head, or more accurately, my heart said, *Are you out of your friggin' mind!?*

I was already under a great deal of stress and making lives easier for others was not what I needed to do right now. Now was the time I needed to put me and my mental well-being first. So, after a long pause, I told him that my preferred name is Erin, and my pronouns are *her* and *she*. He had a one-word response, *Done.* Once again, I felt a weight lifted off my shoulders. It was the first time I smiled in days, and within the hour, they changed the name over my bed, and all staff were briefed on my request. The one downside is that the name on my charts and bracelet stayed the same because my legal name and gender had yet to be changed. But at least notations were made, and over the next two weeks, all the staff from the various medical services involved didn't miss a beat. They did an amazing job, of well, doing their job. They made me feel comfortable, reducing as much stress as they could. And it was a good thing because as it turned out, there was a bit of stress to deal with.

I stayed in the hospital for four days waiting for the angiogram, and they were finally able to slot me in. So, off I went. It was late in the day, around five o'clock, and I was to be the last one in the clinic. They wheeled me in and prepped me for the test. The cardiologist was amazing. She was very calm and explained exactly what was going to happen. She stated that she read my file and spoke with one of my other cardiologists and outlined the procedure. They were going to insert a very long tube into an artery in my wrist and move the tube until it reached the arteries of my heart. They would then inject a dye and take an x-ray showing the blood flow in my arteries and heart. This would uncover any issues, such as blockages in my arteries. They would do the right side and then the left side. She suspected they wouldn't find anything and likely refer me to a gastroenterologist, and that would be it. Or, if they did find something, it would be very minor, they would insert a stent, and again, that would be it. She began the procedure.

They scanned the right side of my heart first. She said everything was clear, and there was no problem. Then she began the scan for the left side. This took a bit more time. At first, there was silence. Then she called a colleague over to look at the scan. After a few moments of debate, she indicated she wanted to consult another surgeon who just came out of surgery. Okay, this wasn't good. I'm not very knowledgeable about medicine, especially cardiology, but even I knew this was not a good thing.

The other surgeon came over and introduced himself. He began reviewing the scans; from the way I was positioned, I couldn't see the scan screens, but I could see the faces of the doctors. That was all I needed to see. As the surgeon watched the screens, his eyes widened.

He then looked down at me at said,
"Oh dear, you're not going to make it through the night!
You need open heart surgery - now."

This is not what I was expecting! I was not prepared to hear that - not in the least. My mind was spinning. He kept talking, so I didn't have time to say anything which didn't matter, because I didn't know what to say.

He told me that they were going to take me to the Cardiac Intensive Care Unit, give me a mild sedative, some blood thinners, and keep me comfortable. They were prepared to do the operation immediately but preferred to wait until morning as his team just completed a long surgery and needed some rest. He assured me they were available at a moment's notice any time during the night. They made the decision, and that was that. That's when I lost it. I began to cry, and then sob uncontrollably. The cardiologists did their best to keep me calm. They reassured me that I was in the right place, under excellent care, and that they weren't going to let anything happen to me overnight.

So, I was immediately taken to the Cardiac Intensive Care Unit and hooked up to IVs while being closely monitored. Fortunately, my daughters joined me at this point, and that was extremely comforting. The surgeon came back in to check on me and gave me the rundown of what was going on. I had Atypical Angina, hence the lack of typical symptomology. He explained precisely what the surgery and recovery process entailed. It was a bit like drinking from a fire hose – everything was coming at me quickly and all at once, and I was somewhat overwhelmed. Fortunately, my youngest daughter took notes and asked clarifying questions; I think just as much for my benefit as for hers.

Next, I was totally surprised by a visit from my ex-wife. For this, I am forever grateful. Not only because she took the time to stop by, but also because she is a profoundly skilled medical professional, especially in cardiology. She knew who the surgeon was, she was able to speak their language, and she translated it all for me. It was comforting. Thank you.

To say I was scared is an understatement. I was terrified. My mind, even under mild sedation, was spinning. I looked at my daughters and began to cry. I wasn't ready to leave my girls. I wanted and needed to be around for them for a very long time. I then began to get angry. I needed to be around for me, for Erin. I'll be damned if I did all of this, blew up my family and endured decades of pain, only not to become my authentic self. I became defiant. I was determined to make it through this for all of us. I was NOT about to be denied.

The next morning, at 7:00 a.m., I was prepared and taken down to the ER waiting area with my youngest daughter by my side. That was so awesome. She was able to keep me calm, which was a great help. Long story short, the surgery was successful, although there were a few complications. The result was that I had to be on life support for about 30 hours from the start of surgery, which they hadn't expected at all. But it all worked out. For the following two weeks, during my recovery in the hospital, my daughters spent as much time as they could with me. My ex checked in on a few occasions as well. Again, acting as my interpreter, which was certainly, above and beyond the call of duty.

The great bonus is that there were no issues with my gender identity during my entire hospitalization. Not one member of my medical team misgendered me or used my old name. They consciously referred to my correct gender and used my correct name at all times. For that, I am thankful because it greatly reduced my stress levels by not triggering my dysphoria. Stress over the years is why I was in this situation in the first place, so I appreciated their awareness. But, as much as they supported me, the time came to plan for my discharge and recovery, and suddenly, reality came knocking - very loudly.

At this time, I realized I was going to be doing this on my own. I was going to be alone, at my home recovering from major, life-saving, open-heart surgery. I wondered how I was going to make that work. I was fortunate that my daughters were able to spend some time with me, but they had things they needed to do. My ex stopped in occasionally to check on me and help with our dog, and I had wonderful neighbours who dropped off some meals. All of this was so amazing, and I was fortunate and thankful for all of it, but I did experience trepidation, knowing I was basically by myself.

I was on my own for the majority of the three-month recovery period. I occupied most of the time doing my physical therapy that consisted of getting up and walking around the house, caring for the surgical site, doing breathing exercises, and other daily self-care tasks. I made my meals and took care of my dog, whose company was extremely comforting, and distracted me in a good way. The rest of the time was spent in bed or on the couch trying to get comfortable and watching TV. The worst part was at night.

Trying to sleep was almost impossible. The first issue was that I had to sleep on my back, which is not something I can do. I'm a side sleeper. But, that was not permitted because it put stress on my sternum which was completely cut in half for the surgery. It was held together by titanium wire until the bone could heal and grow back together. Second, nighttime is when my mind would, once again, wander. I was paranoid that something would happen to me, and I would need to call 9-1-1. I always made sure the front door was unlocked, and the alarm system was off so that emergency services could get in easily. I was now sleeping in the unsecured home I created, so that also kept me awake.

The last concern I had was thinking about getting up out of bed. That was an adventure because I was not able to use my arms to push me up. The only way to get out of bed each morning was to, essentially, do a sit-up. I was very weak due to the surgery, and my core was not in the best of shape to start with. Some days, it took me ten minutes to get out of bed as I tried to do it without putting stress on my chest and experiencing pain. I always managed it somehow. It became pure determination because I decided I was going to get through this.

February 29, 2016

Had a bit of a moment, actually I think you could call it a minor meltdown. The good old 1:00 in the morning, brain goes to a stupid place again. It wasn't so much about transitioning, more around my physical health. The diagnosis and surgery happened relatively quickly, so I didn't have much time to digest it. In retrospect, that was probably a good thing. From the time they ran the final diagnostic test to when I was in the OR was 16 hours. So, I really wasn't able to process what was happening. And during my recovery, I was really working hard on being strong for my girls so that they were not panicking.

I think my brain finally caught up with all that in one night. I thought I was taking good care of myself, very physically active (runner, dive master) ate well, not overweight, not diabetic, nonsmoker, not a big drinker, no high blood pressure. But still, at my age to have open heart surgery, what does this mean for the rest of my life? It didn't last long, probably 20 minutes, but I think it was just time to let go and get it out of my system. In is interesting how transitioning took a back seat to all of this.

With some assistance from friends and family, I kept improving. The day I was able to climb all the way up the stairs to my bedroom without stopping was a feat to be celebrated - my goodness, how everything became reduced to the basics. I eventually graduated from doing indoor circuits, walking slowly around my house for exercise, to being able to go outside for walks. Fortunately, the sidewalks were not icy, allowing me to do this. It took me four times longer than usual just to walk around the block, but at least I was able to get some fresh air and feel the sun on my face. I had a routine and started feeling a bit better, growing a sense that I was going to be okay. I believed I was going to make it through this. But, as they say, life is what happens when you try to make plans. Once again, things went a bit sideways.

March 14, 2016

Life is interesting. Just when you think you are starting to get your feet back underneath you, in my case quite literally, something else is thrown in your path. Today, I lost my very best friend of 15 years.

She was always glad to see me, seemed to know when I needed a nudge or just some companionship. And always, always, made me smile. Well today, she passed away. We were there for each other and watched each other "grow up" so to speak. Her, physically, me emotionally, to become who I was meant to be. And since I have been on my own for the past year, she was my go-to companion. She was my 15-year-old yellow Labrador Retriever, Abby. Abigail when she was in trouble, but none the less my very true friend. I loved her and miss her like crazy.

The house is now very quiet without her. It is going to take quite a while to get used to. I swear I see her out of the corner of my eye, lying on her bed, waiting for me to give her a rub, or take her outside to sniff and explore. It has been a very lonely day. I know she is in a better place, and I will be okay, it's just, well, it's just hard. Rest in peace Abby, I miss you so much.

Abby's passing was not sudden as she was getting up there in years, especially for a Lab, but that didn't make it any easier. No matter how much I thought I might be prepared for something like this, I really wasn't. She seemed to know that I needed her immediately following the surgery, but once she saw I was going to be okay, she decided it was her time. My ex-wife stepped in to help with all the details as I was in no shape to deal with it on my own. Once again, thank you. I took a long time to adjust to the quiet and the sense of loss and loneliness. Many times, I walked in the door after my daily walks, and I called her name out of habit, only to realize she wasn't coming. I eventually adjusted and moved forward.

Eventually, I was able to feel well enough to welcome more friends into my home as they asked if they could stop by for short visits. My boss stopped in a few times, along with neighbours and members of my dive team. It was good to reconnect with the outside world and maintain meaningful friendships. Life started feeling a bit normal, like I finally turned a corner. I began getting out more and actually drove short distances because I was now able to wear a seat belt across my chest. I managed to do some small errands, so things were looking up. That's when life decided it was time for yet another curveball.

My car decided to give up - flat out, dead. It needed replacing. I certainly did not plan for that in any way. So, I needed to get a new car. I reviewed my financial situation, figured out what my budget was and went from there. The search began, and I was fortunate to find a used car at the dealership I was familiar with from past purchases. They were able to set me up with something that worked for me, given my circumstances. Most times, I chose to think this can be an exciting thing or this can be a fun thing to do. At least, it usually was for me. But not this time. This became just another stressor at a time when it was the last thing I needed. I had enough to deal with over the past few months, or so I thought. But, I was determined to get through it and move on. After a while, I did come to like my car and started getting back on track with my life. But, of course, there was one more thing that came my way.

It was just shortly after solving the car issue that I received notification my ex-wife was filing for divorce - deep breath. Now, I have to admit that this should not have come as a surprise. Being separated for a year is the minimum time required by law for separation before you can file for divorce. It was just not something that was on the top of my mind. I lost track of time regarding this, given all I dealt with. But it was a reality I had to face. I think it was knowing this was the end, that we were going to be legally divorced. I was going to be on my own going forward in my life, and I felt the finality of it all.

I made it this far. I had emergency open-heart surgery, and

I was still here. My faithful companion passed away, and I was still here. My car crapped out, and I was still here. Now, I was going to be officially on my own, and I was still here. It was a realization that life was worthwhile, that it was worth the effort, whatever it took, regardless of what it threw at me. I was resilient and achieving more strength by committing to my authentic self. I became even more determined to get through all of this. Again, I was not going to be denied. I became very focused on my goal of completing my journey. I wanted to continue finding me, and I was so close. The little things that went south were no longer an issue or a barrier, but instead, they were just that - little things.

My mantra became, *If it isn't life-threatening, move on.* Perspective is a wonderful thing, and yet, it can be a difficult thing to have. It took so much to find a clear perspective at such a great cost, and I wasn't about to let all that go to waste. It was a tough battle, and battle is not too strong a word. I was more determined to move forward, to focus on the big things in life like family, close friends and helping others. And, of course, I wanted and needed to focus on me, to celebrate all my small victories, and be thankful for what I had. It finally looked like I was going to beat Gender Dysphoria and have my gender match internally and externally. I realize that this is something the vast majority of people don't have to worry about or deal with, and I hope that everyone can celebrate who they are, just as I do.

For the first time, I was facing life from a position of strength. I was slowly taking control of the bus on the road of my life. This was a good thing as I prepared to take another big step, deciding to come out entirely at work. I took another deep breath.

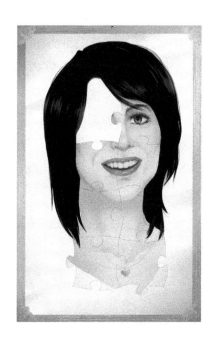

Acceptance

Thursday June 2, 2016, 3:32 p.m.
Email from the Dean

Personal Announcement:

I am writing to share a personal announcement on behalf of one of our Smith staff members. A few months ago, our colleague E. LeBlanc confided in me that he had been struggling with a medical situation for a very long time, Gender Dysphoria. People born with Gender Dysphoria have an incongruence between their internal gender identity and their external physical identity.

He was diagnosed with Gender Dysphoria years ago and is in the process of aligning his external identity to match his internal gender identity assigned at birth. On a go forward basis our coworker will be known as Erin Leeann LeBlanc. Her preferred pronouns are her, she and Ms.

I am happy for Erin and pleased she is comfortable sharing her true self with the people who work and study at Smith. Please join me in supporting and welcoming our new, old friend Erin Leeann LeBlanc to Smith! Many of you may have questions, are curious, or simply would like to show your support for Erin. Below is a letter from Erin that may answer some of your questions and tells part of Erin's story.

Erin's Story:

To: Faculty and Staff, Smith School of Business

From: Erin LeBlanc

I am writing to you to share something that is deeply personal that is occurring in my life. Seventeen years ago, I was given a medical diagnosis that was potentially life altering. At that time, I thought I was strong enough to work my way through it and decided not to pursue any course of action. After years of struggling, I was reassessed just over a year ago and the diagnosis was confirmed. I have Gender Dysphoria. So, what does that mean? It means that I am Transgender. My internal identity does not match my physical body. I have made the decision to transition and gain congruity between my inner and outer self, for the first time in my life. To be the woman I was meant to be.

When I think about living my life as the "old" me, I am filled with dread. For all of my life, I have looked in the mirror only to see a stranger looking back. I can no longer live a lie. I need to be true to myself and my family, to live an authentic life. Hence my decision. Please know that this is not a lifestyle choice. This is something that I was born with. No one would choose this. I am doing this because I have to, not because I want to. I can no longer deny who I am. So, I have made the decision to survive. This has not been an easy decision and has not been without cost. However, I know that it is the only path for me.

I am very fortunate in that I have the unconditional support of my two exceptional daughters, and my family including my brother and his family along with my sister and her family. My neighbours and friends continue to stand with me. My colleagues at my volunteer activities couldn't be more supportive and happier that I finally can be who I really am. I have been able to surround myself with a team of professionals that are looking after my physical and emotional well-being. My two primary care doctors, my endocrinologist, my general therapist, my gender therapist, and athletic therapist are completely on board and providing me with outstanding care. I have been on a medical protocol for a year and every aspect is being monitored and is going according to expectations. I am well looked after!

All I want to do is live my life, do my job and contribute to the community — to be able to live, love, and laugh, as me. I know that this is not going to be a "walk in the park". Not every day is a good day, but I am filled with hope, and I do what I can each day to make it a good day. And, now, there are more good days than bad days. I wake up every morning looking forward to starting the day, to experience my new life.

This is all to say that I will be my authentic self-starting Monday,

June 6. I know that you may have questions and may be trying to wrap your head around all of this. I understand that. I have been very forthcoming with everyone in my life. I am happy to answer any and all questions that you have. As one of my mentors reminds me, life is short and you're dead a long time. I will no longer live a life of regret, but one of hope, happiness and authenticity, every day, for the rest of my life. I hope that each of us can continue to do this, together.

Erin Leeann LeBlanc

It was done. This email went out to everyone, over 300 staff and faculty in my department, from our Dean. Prior to this and once I was back to work after recovering from my heart surgery, there was so much to do. There were many moving pieces to manage, and I was fortunate to have many people supporting me doing a ton of work.

I met with my boss and our HR manager to start working through many of the details. The first thing to figure out was the communication plan. I informed them I wanted to have several in-person conversations with key influencers and long-time friends in our department before the email went out. My reasons for this were multi-fold. I didn't want these people to find out about my transition via email. I wanted to have a face-to-face conversation to discuss this very personal decision. I also wanted to give them the time they required to digest the information and allow for follow up conversations if required. And, it was important they had time to educate themselves on the topic if needed. This would provide them with knowledge to address concerns from their staff as the first line of support once the email went out.

The second thing to do was to finalize the date to *flip the switch* as it were. I chose Monday, June 6, for a few reasons. Mostly, because this was the Monday after the Friday, my youngest daughter was going to graduate from university. It was a special day, and I wanted to be there as her dad. That was important to her, and I wanted to be able to do that for her. It was going to be extra special because I was going to be the one to convey the degree to her when she walked across the stage. As a faculty member, I applied for and received permission from the university secretariat to be able to do this. I graduated with my master's in law at this same university, which meant a lot for both of us. I am so thankful I could do this, and I will always remember that day as a very proud parent.

Next, we had to work backwards to select a date for the email to drop. I decided it would be on the Thursday before graduation and the start to the weekend. There was some rationale for that decision. The plan was that I leave work on Thursday at 3:00 p.m. The email would go out from the Dean shortly after that. I would not be at work the next day. I was going to take the Friday off to attend and participate in my daughter's graduation. I also wanted people at work to have a day to digest the contents of the email. I wanted to give them a day to have the OMG and WTF moments without worrying about running into me. I also wanted them to have a chance to speak with their department heads and supervisors if they chose to. As I stated earlier, I had decades to deal with this in my head; it wasn't reasonable to assume everyone could wrap their heads around all of this in a few days. Hence, the plan.

The other thing I wanted to do was include a picture of me, Erin, in the announcement. Once again, there is a reason for this. My biggest fear was that they would be thinking, *Oh boy, this is going to be interesting, a dude in a dress!* I needed to combat that. Especially with a weekend in between the announcement and when I showed up for work on Monday. I didn't want them conjuring up images of *Mrs. Doubtfire* or Dustin Hoffman in *Tootsie*. After all, that is probably the only reference most people have. So that was the plan.

This meant I had to have a photo done. Everyone in my little circle was on board. My boss suggested we use the same photographer who did all the pictures for the staff and faculty web profiles. She told me the department was happy to pay for the photo session. I was so fortunate! I wanted a professional photo that fit in with everyone else with the same background and style, and not different from theirs. So, we booked the photoshoot for a few weeks before the notice was going out. It was done early in the evening after work in my building when no one was around. I told the photographer why I was getting my picture done, and she was super excited! We had a wonderful time and got some great shots to choose from. I was thankful I was able to do this. It made me feel much more secure about the whole coming out *event*. The next steps followed.

I had a group meeting with all the staff in my office regarding my transition. I never doubted they would support me, but when they didn't hesitate in doing so, it was such a relief. This is an excellent group of people and I was fortunate to be part of such an incredible team. Following our meeting and over the next three weeks, I had twenty one-on-one conversations with key individuals within the school. Each separate meeting was about an hour long, and I did most on my own. There were a few where either my boss or our HR manager attended to support me. I wasn't quite sure what reaction I would receive, but as it turned out, it was completely unnecessary. Without exception, every person was super understanding and accepting. While they were all surprised, they were also very happy for me. It was a stressful process, mostly due to not knowing what the reactions would be, but it was also very validating. I knew this was something I needed to do, and every person's response reiterated that I was going to be okay.

Next, we had to review all the places in the numerous systems involved in the institution's administration where I had to change my name and gender. The trick was that there were only a limited number of places this was able to be done without legal documentation. Things like email addresses, directory listings, web profiles, staff ID, business cards, and office signs could all easily be changed. However, more official accounts, such as payroll, pension, and other financial records, could not be altered until my name officially changed with the Social Insurance office - that record of official documentation from the government. I recognized this as a longer process and that I had to wait. So, we went to work on the list of what was able to be done right away.

It was an interesting process, to say the least. The good news is that the organization had policies in place to address these types of things. The bad news is that it had never been put to the test yet, so the processes to support the policies were not in place. This is something we had to do, and I worked together with all the departments. We noted what we did and how we did it, so that it would be easier next time. There was now a process in place because we knew there would be a next time. We knew it was not going to be a case of if someone else was to come out, but rather, when. The silver lining to all this is that everyone was extremely empathetic as to why the changes had to be made. They all wanted to be collaborative but just didn't know how to do it or if it could be done. I tried to remain patient, but I must admit that after a while, it did wear me down.

There are only so many times you can hear,
"I'm not sure that can be done,"
before you start to get frustrated.

It was like death by a thousand cuts. Individually, it's not such a big deal. But to hear it over and over and over again for a week, it became a different story. Regardless, we kept moving forward and crossed things off our to-do list. By the end of it all, everyone was ready to go for when we flipped the switch, and before I knew it, the time had come.

On Thursday, June 2, at three o'clock, I walked out of my office for the last time as the old me. It is something I will never forget. All the staff in my office were lined up outside my door to say goodbye to the old me one last time. It was so incredibly thoughtful. Needless to say, I totally lost it and broke down. I wasn't expecting it at all. For all of them to take the time to do this and express how much they cared for me, made my heart feel so good. And then, off I went.

I went straight home, and shortly after I left, the email with the announcement went out. Before I even made it to my house to check my inbox, I could tell the email dropped because my smartphone starting buzzing with incoming notifications. Over the next few hours, I received over 100 emails. I held my breath as I opened each one. It was an afternoon and evening filled with tears - tears of relief and happiness because every single one was so positive and supportive. I spent the rest of the evening and the next day replying to each and every one. It was the least I could do.

Hi Erin,

There are no words to express how courageous you are. I'm incredibly moved at how forthcoming you've been about what you've gone through. The bravery it must have took to share this with us, and the world, is astounding. You are a beautiful person, inside and out, and I hope you know that I am strongly and squarely in your corner. Can't wait to see you in person to give you a big hug!

Hi Erin,

I am blown away by this news but in the most positive way possible. Thank you for sharing your story and letting us be a part of your journey. This is such an inspirational story and you are a true role model for anyone who is going through or is fighting with Gender Dysphoria. You have great courage and strength and should be very proud of yourself.

Hi Erin

Sending you ONE BIG FAT HUG ERIN!!! I'm so proud of you. And as I said before should you need anything, support, whatever you can always count on me. We've had 12 good years working together and I can't wait to work with you Erin for the remainder of our time here. You are truly a strong individual for taking this step to becoming who you are supposed to be. You truly are an inspiring individual.

Hi Erin,

I just read the email from the Dean and wanted to tell you what a strong and courageous person I think you are. I cannot fathom what you have gone through over the last 17 years and I am so happy that you made the decision to survive and to be your true, beautiful self. Amazing.

Dear Erin,

Thank you for sharing your story. It is deeply touching. I cannot imagine what you have been through these past few years, but I am relieved to know that you have decided to put all this behind you and be the person whom you really are. There is no playbook to guide someone through such a life changing transition, but this is the right thing to do. I want you to know that you can count on my friendship and on my unconditional support.

Erin,

Welcome aboard. I know this must have been a very difficult decision to make, wondering how it would be accepted by your peers, colleagues and friends. I would like to think that I qualify as each of these and I will say that I am whole-heartedly behind you. I admire your courage and I am prepared to do everything in my power to support you as you move forward. Please do not hesitate to reach out to me if there is anything that I can do to help.

Erin,

I want to say how incredibly happy I am for you to be able to now live your full life at last, to be able to take a deep breath every morning and to be able to be who you are. I am also so sad that you must have been in so much pain for so long...but knowing what a strong, good, courageous and optimistic person you are, I know the path ahead for you is a happy one. You are simply awesome.

Hi Erin,

I know you don't "begin" until Monday, but I think we can begin welcoming you right now! I mentioned to my wife last night how brave I thought your decision was, and she corrected me – she said, "Think of how difficult it has been for her for all of these years until now!" I suspect she has it right. I can't imagine what you've gone through/are going through, but I only wish you the best and look forward to working with you.

Erin hi there,

I wanted to email and say how sorry I am that you have had to struggle for so long. I hope that going forward, you can experience all the joy, fulfillment and health you so obviously deserve.

Dear Erin,

Radiance and joy – that is what I first noticed when I saw your photo. Courage, strength, admiration, inspiration, determination, daring greatly, vulnerability, authenticity – these are the words that came flooding into my head as I read your personal story and announcement. I am so so so happy for you. I hope that your first week of being your authentic self has been wonderful and all that you hoped so far. I have been thinking about you a lot. I am also filled with hope and pride for our institution and workplace. It was heartening to read that you have been receiving so much support from your colleagues. Well done for taking that step and setting an example for us all.

Erin,

Just wanted to let you know the response has been overwhelmingly supportive. We have a great group of people here that care for you a great deal. Lots of tears as people learned of your struggle but happiness that you have had the strength to be who you are. Very happy and proud of you, can't wait until Monday.

And it went on and on. Now I really knew I was going to be okay. Another huge sigh of relief.

The next day came and went with the highlight of the year being my youngest daughter's graduation. Yes, I am a proud parent for sure. It was not an easy time for her with everything going on with me and our family; such a great accomplishment on her part. Fortunately, I was able to take her out for lunch following the ceremony for which I was very thankful. She was heading back to where she worked, and I cherished every second I could have with her.

That evening, things started to settle down. The emails pretty much stopped, and the excitement of the day calmed. I decided I was going to go and get my ears pierced, so off I went. That was an amusing event. I arrived at the store and stated I would like to get my ears pierced. She asked if I was getting additional piercings. Nope. She directed me to the chair and examined my earlobes. She asked if I was there because the holes grew over. Nope. As a result, she was very careful, checking to make sure I was okay, and offering to give me time after the first one to relax if I was uncomfortable with the pain. It became clear she was confused that a woman my age had not had their ears pierced by now and assumed I was concerned about it being painful. It was quite comical, while at the same time, providing further validation of my authentic self.

It was such an emotional few days, and to say I was exhausted is an understatement. The weekend went by with lots of time to relax and being able to be my authentic self everywhere and full-time provided me with extreme liberation. For the first time, I knew how the majority of the rest of the world feels, and I suspect takes for granted. And, of course, they would because they would have no reason to know what it's like to suffer from Gender Dysphoria, thank goodness. It was surreal that all I had to do was just be me!! The next step? I had to show up on Monday morning for the first time as Erin...

Once again, I took a deep breath. I stepped out of the elevator and went through the glass doors into our office suite. I received a warm welcome from the staff who had already arrived, but nothing over the top. They provided me with just the typical greeting as if nothing was different. It was perfect! I got to my office, and the sign outside my office was changed with my correct name, *Erin L. LeBlanc*. My name tag and new business cards were waiting on my desk, and both were correct. I logged into my computer, and my email address was updated. Someone made arrangements to make sure it was all ready to go when the time came. It was amazing.

To the outside world around me, the rest of the day was uneventful. It seemed like just another Monday with the usual few meetings and work being done; no one missed a beat. Well actually, a handful of people did stop in to give me a hug and some flowers. So, okay, maybe not 100 percent normal, but it was relatively calm. In saying that, it wasn't a normal day for me. It was a bit surreal in a way because it felt so beautiful to be at peace finally.

After being in a place that was the source of so many anxiety attacks and frustration, I now felt comfortable for the first time in a long time, if not ever. As the day went on, I experienced more and more validation for who I was.

This was not the end of the process, not at all. Next on the list was all the paperwork required to change my name and gender legally. This was a personal decision, and for various reasons, not everyone who transitions takes these steps. It is up to each of us to decide what resonates with us, and I definitely wanted all my documentation to state who I am as Erin correctly. This included things like my driver's license, health card, birth certificate, passport, and all my banking and personal financial accounts. For me, all of these changes were predicated on obtaining an official government-issued change of name document. As it turns out, that was easier said than done.

Living in Canada, I had to apply for a change of name in the province where I resided. It involved submitting several documents, including a police criminal background check and a copy of my birth certificate. The 17-page form was initially daunting but working through it was not as difficult as it first appeared. I also had to get a guarantor, someone who knew me, was a professional, and could attest to the fact I lived in Ontario for at least 12 months. Fortunately for me, I know a lot of lawyers, so that was easy.

I discovered that when applying for a name change, the request is published in The Ontario Gazette provincial publication for anyone to see. However, if transgender and the name change is for the purpose to match correct gender, one can apply for the publication not to occur. I did not hesitate to apply for this option because the purpose is to prevent the potential for harassment or harm when the name change becomes public knowledge. I sent off the completed paperwork, and some weeks later, my name change certificate arrived. Oh, happy day!!! This was the first domino I needed to fall for the remainder of all the changes to come to fruition.

Armed with this, I was able to change my name on all

my financial information at work, at banks, with the utility companies, and on my land registrar for land deeds. I didn't realize just how many places this had to be done - even things like affinity cards such as Airmiles and other store client cards. Some were easy, and some, not so much. Everything at work was easy, as well as with the banks. Some utilities took a bit more work, but they got done. The most difficult by far was my driver's license and health card.

Both of these required a visit to a local, provincial transportation office. The name change was easy as I had my change of name document; change of gender was a different story. Because I was not born in Ontario, I had to apply for a name and gender change for my birth certificate in the province of Quebec because that was where I was born. This was a lengthy procedure, and I wanted to make as many changes as I could as quickly as I could. As it turns out, Ontario, at the time, didn't need my birth certificate changed to reflect my correct gender if I was able to produce a letter from a licensed physician who was treating me. The physician needed to acknowledge that my change in *designated sex* - their word, not mine, which should be *gender*, but I digress - was appropriate. I also needed to write a letter stating why I wanted to change my gender indicators to my correct gender on my driver's license, auto ownership, and provincial health card. Armed with all this, I went to the local office.

Well, apparently, I was the only one who knew of this alternative to a providing an updated birth certificate to change my gender. While my name change was handled with no problem, I was initially denied having my gender changed because I did not have a new birth certificate. I told the clerk I had two letters to take its place. He said that making the change was not possible, and after a 10-minute debate in a very public setting, I was getting nowhere, and yes, I was totally outed as a trans person as a result. Finally, a supervisor overheard the discussion and joined in. Initially, she concurred with the clerk until I stated that according to information on their website, I could use the documentation I provided to change my gender marker. After a brief time, the supervisor left us to check. She returned a few moments later and told the clerk, *Yes, he is correct, go ahead and make the change.* Not only did she misgender me in a public setting, but she also provided no apology. I was livid but tried to remain calm. I was trying to pick my battles, and I wanted the changes made, so for the most part, I sucked it up. But it was terrible. I hope having experienced this that they are clear about what the process is so, others will not have to go through this discomfort and humiliation.

Thinking the worst was over, I was sadly mistaken. The change of gender on my birth certificate tested my limits for sure. I was able to find information regarding the process on the Quebec Provincial Ministry website. It clearly stated that the Province of Quebec is the only body able to make changes on a birth certificate issued in Quebec. Okay, fine. There was the required paperwork I needed to complete, along with letters from my physicians and healthcare providers indicating that the change in sex designation to F on my birth certificate was appropriate. Fortunately for me, my gender therapist was well versed in this process and prepared everything for me. I, in turn, gathered all the required documentation, and it was ready to go. The sticky point was that I was not a current resident of Quebec. I had to prove that I was not living in Quebec at the time, and that was easy. Then came the speed bump as they told me I needed a letter from the appropriate ministry in Ontario, stating that it was not able to change my sex designation on my Quebec birth certificate.

Wait a minute - didn't I just read that the Province of Quebec was the only one that could make changes? So why did I need a letter from a Ministry in Ontario stating that same thing? Confused, I made a few phone calls and asked this exact question. I repeated that it was clear on their website that only Quebec could do it, so why did I need a letter? Three more phone calls and the message was the same each time, *get the letter*. Fine!

I had no idea what ministry in Ontario to contact, and I wasn't about to waste a bunch of time bouncing around from department to department trying to figure it out. I decided to contact my elected provincial parliament representative to get some assistance. This, I must say, was amazing because, within 10 days, I had the letter in my hands. I am so appreciative given that governments are not always known for supporting the transgender community, but in this instance, they provided excellent service. So, armed with all the appropriate documents, I submitted the completed application. A few months later, my new birth certificate with my correct name and gender arrived. This was a very momentous occasion.

All that remained was a new passport and Social Insurance Number identification. This was so easy compared to the preceding bureaucracy. I completed the paperwork, obtained the required endorsements from guarantors, went to the appropriate federal offices and it was done. There were no issues. Seeing my new passport was extra special. I am fortunate to have had opportunities to travel the world, and I love to travel, so having the correct documentation was very important.

There are so many things a person has to do to transition legally, and it can be frustrating and exhausting. Every step along the way I was challenged to prove who I was and justify why I wanted something so simple like basic documentation to reflect my correct name and gender. I didn't think it was too much to ask for, and it made me realize that it's no wonder so many people in the community experience depression and anxiety due to all these roadblocks.

We have to be prepared to battle every step along the way. We must prepare for the worst and hope for the best.

This process is something the cisgender world may not be aware of, and that needs to be recognized and not taken for granted.

It is exhausting, both emotionally and physically. I always say that this is not for the faint of heart, but rather, for the strong and courageous. Trans people are just that, strong and courageous. We have to be. But it can wear you down. Again, this can be death by a thousand cuts just because we want to be our authentic selves and because we choose to survive. Who would go through all of this as a lifestyle choice? On top of everything else I had going on in my life, why would I suddenly choose to be transgender? How absurd.

I still had one more thing to do to complete my journey.

Joy

January 16, 2018

I'm done. Finished. Nothing else left to do. It was the only surgery that I'm having. I am living my life as my authentic self, as the woman I have always been, finally having complete congruity between my internal and external self.

Since coming out at work, I spent the rest of the summer of 2017 focusing on just trying to establish and get comfortable with my new normal. I was busy with work, which was going well. In a way, it was odd that I was getting more and more requests for consulting and speaking engagements regarding diversity and supporting the transgender community. Different organizations across the province and in other parts of Canada wanted me to address their gatherings and tell my story. Along with this, all the work we did preparing for me to come out at work paid off. I was fortunate, along with my colleague in HR, to receive an award from Queen's University. It was in recognition of creating processes assisting people who plan to transition and identifying and removing barriers for transgender people in the workplace.

Instead of losing work, as is the case for many who transition, I received more work than I could handle. I was shocked and humbled by that. But I just kept on doing what I could do because I wanted to make it easier for those behind me. I owe a considerable debt to those who went before me, and I felt it was time for me to pay it forward. They were the pioneers and the ones who risked so much more than I in their attempt to be authentic. Many were bullied, mistreated, maligned, ignored, and even attacked. Because of their bravery and their work, I was able to progress in much more favourable circumstances. I send a heartfelt thank you to all of them.

I worked hard on getting out and socializing. And, I spent as much time as I could with my girls whenever the opportunity came up. I could never get enough time with my daughters - what parent does? They were doing a bit better with the divorce and transition, but it was still a struggle at times. It made me sad and, quite frankly, angry. I was angry with myself for being the cause of what those I loved were going through. I tried to convince myself that I was really the same person, just now more myself. And I admit, I did believe that. But, now I see that there was so much more to all of this, and it was totally wrong to focus just on me.

I was different during and after my transition. I was too caught up on *everything Erin*. When I look back, I realize that I was not practicing great parenting because my daughters saw me differently than I did. I still had the same quirking sense of humour, the same opinions and thoughts on many issues, and mostly, the same likes and preferences. I thought I was essentially the same person on the inside, but I now realize that my perception of me was very different from my daughters' perception of who I had transitioned to. I wish I realized this sooner. It would have provided more accurate insight as to what my daughters were going through. It all makes sense now; of course, I was not the same person to them. I looked different, sounded different, and in some cases, my personality changed. I was more engaged, more present, more talkative and, quite frankly, happier. I think that was because the depression and Gender Dysphoria didn't control me any longer. I wish I had been more aware of this at the time, so I could have been more sensitive and understood that, in some ways, they were grieving the loss of their father. In hindsight, I don't know how I didn't see that. Well, that's not true. If I'm honest, it's called being too self-absorbed. I am so sorry.

I know that one doesn't take this journey to transition in isolation. I have been saying that for years. Yet, for some reason, that was lost on me in some ways. I knew I had to give everyone else time to work this out. I knew I had to answer all the questions. I knew I had to be strong and positive, but I forgot to see things from their true perspective. I've made a note to do that with everything in my life and everyone in my circle.

The other thing that occupied a lot of my time was getting the prep work done for my final transition surgery. The procedure is known by a few names. The most popular of which appear to be Gender Reassignment Surgery (GRS), Gender Confirmation Surgery (GCS), or Gender Affirmation Surgery (GAS). For many years, this type of surgery was known as Sexual Reassignment Surgery (SRS). These are really generic terms for several different types of surgeries depending on one's type of transition, whether male to female (M2F) or female to male (F2M).

Personally, I always had a preference to use either GCS or GAS, and yes, that second one is an unfortunate acronym, but it is what it is. For me GRS doesn't make sense as I don't feel I am reassigning my gender. I have always been a woman and was born that way. I just had a physical birth defect of having male anatomy. This surgery was confirmation or affirmation of my gender as a woman. The difference may be subtle, but it isn't for me. Some may disagree, and that's ok. As I said, everyone's circumstances and journeys are different. We are unique individuals, and as such, so is our transition.

I made plans for this to take place as soon as possible at a well-established and world-renowned clinic specializing in transgender surgeries. People from all over the world go to this clinic. Located in Montreal, only three hours by train for me, it was the most convenient location, which was a bonus.

Fortunately, my gender therapist was extremely familiar with the surgeons and the clinic and their processes. She was able to do all the paperwork for me to apply for the surgery, which was a massive burden off my shoulders. With all the forms and requisite authorizations complete, all I could do was wait for the call with a date for my surgery. The waiting time for this clinic at one time was two years! However, they expanded their facilities and added another surgeon, so that time was reduced to eight months. It still seemed like an eternity. I waited.

I had the summer to establish a routine and settle into my life. One thing I wanted to do was expand my circle of friends in a new environment. I decided to go to the water, a place that has always been a source of peace for me. I found a small boat just the right size for one person that was very seaworthy and in good shape. I was fortunate to be able to live on that boat for part of the summer, which was exactly what I needed. To settle in on it for weeks at a time was one of the best decisions I made post coming out. Regardless of the weather, I enjoyed every minute of it and spent a great deal of time reflecting on my life and what I had to look forward to.

During that time, I made some wonderful new friends, lifelong friends. We spent so much time just hanging out together. When I wasn't with them, I was happy on this little boat curled up on the couch with a book or watching a movie. It was a great balance of connecting with others, as well as myself. Regardless of the circumstances, I was just as happy to be in my own company as I was with others. This was really a first for me, and I realized that when I'm content in my own skin, it doesn't matter where I am or who I'm with. That was a major breakthrough for me.

The best part is that I didn't have to be concerned about anyone knowing I was transgender. No one knew me prior to this. There was no history to overcome. This was the first time they were meeting me and getting to know me. And no one, absolutely no one, had any issues with me. Some had an inkling and guessed, but that didn't make any difference to them. None at all. In fact, one of the couples who had belonged to the marina for about 20 years knew about me after reading a few of my Facebook posts. They wanted to learn more about Gender Dysphoria and transgender, so we had some great conversations. They told me that if anyone at the marina had a problem with me, they would have to deal with them! Alrighty then, they had my back! It turns out, that was never needed.

It was nice to be treated as one of the girls, included in

activities and conversations. I always felt welcome, safe, and appreciated. Again, this was a novel sense that was greatly overdue.

To not be dismissed,
and to be recognized for who I really am,
is an incredible feeling.

I am so thankful to all of my friends I met there. It made me think of something I wrote early on in my transition. It was never more true than at this point.

October 4, 2017

I learned how to be the new kid on the block, in my new skin where nobody knew me. No previous history. I forced myself to get out there, to take risks, to learn how to make friends and how to interject myself into an established community. It took time. And yes, I did skin my knees, figuratively speaking. But I continued on. Something I never would have even considered doing prior to my transition.

Then the call came. It was the first week of September, and I received a call from the clinic in Montreal. They had a cancellation in October just four weeks away and asked if I wanted to select that date. Well, that was a stupid question; of course, I did!! I jumped at it. With a bit more paperwork, the date of October 10, 2018 was set. How excited was I? I can't even begin to describe that.

I quickly had a conversation with my boss regarding the sudden acceleration of the date and subsequent recovery time. This was not an issue at all. Once again, the support I received was second to none. So, it was confirmed that I would leave for Montreal on Thanksgiving Monday here in Canada, check-in, and prepare for surgery on the Wednesday. I also had to make arrangements for three months of recovery at home. Once again, I would do this on my own. However, this time, I was more prepared. I did this once before with my open heart surgery, so I was familiar with what I had to do to manage the recovery. Because of this, I was more confident with the entire process and not nearly as afraid or nervous.

Before I knew it, I found myself on the train to Montreal, heading to the clinic. To say that the staff there were accommodating and welcoming is a serious understatement. They took such good care of everything. All I had to do was get myself on the train, and they looked after the rest. When I arrived in Montreal, there was a chauffeur-driven limousine waiting to take me to the pre-surgery accommodation, which was a standard service provided to any patient of the clinic. Once there, I went to my room with instructions about how the process was going to unfold.

There was an underlying bonus; a friend of mine who lived near Toronto was having surgery the same day as me. She didn't know I was also going to be there, and I wanted to surprise her. And surprise her, I did! It was great. It was wonderful to have her there. We had some free time the day before checking into the surgery unit, so we explored Montreal a bit and tried to relax. It was hard to contain our excitement, but the time finally came and we went to the surgery unit the next day very early in the morning. We met the surgeon and other surgical staff; we were all set.

The surgery went well. Recovering was painful, I won't lie about that. But, that was expected, and the staff did their best to make every patient comfortable. There were ten others there for surgery that week, and we all bonded over the common experience. I met some remarkable people from different countries, all of whom made the experience more bearable. It helped to talk about how I felt with people who knew exactly what I was experiencing. We sort of formed our own support group. Make no mistake about it, this was major, invasive surgery. There was nothing easy about it, nothing at all. It was difficult to sleep and getting comfortable enough to eat was a challenge. Just walking down the hallway seemed like an insurmountable task. Although each day did get a little better, I knew it was going to be a long road to full recovery. Once again, this is another aspect that makes transitioning not for the faint of heart.

I had the chance to have a few conversations with my surgeon, who was also part of the management team for the clinic. We talked about the philosophy of the clinic and how it treats the patients. The goal of the clinic is to reduce each patient's level of anxiety as much as possible. This is critical to a healthy recovery. Some people arrive for the first time in Canada, and some with limited English or French language skills. The clinic doesn't want their patients arriving in Montreal by air or train, not knowing where to go or how to get a taxi. This is why the car service was implemented. Dietary restrictions are also honoured and not an issue. The chef meets with each patient to review any special needs and all are accommodated. The entire process is designed to make everything simple and straight forward every step of the way. From my experience, mission accomplished. For many trans people, this could have been the first time they were treated with such dignity and respect, and truly heard. That in and of itself is a great thing, but a sad statement as to how many in the community are often times mistreated. Many thanks to all of the staff there.

Before I knew it, the week-long post-surgery recovery at

the clinic was over, and it was time to go home. Three hours later, I was back home with the help of a friend who picked me up at the station and drove me. It was strange to be in a quiet place with no nursing staff or anyone else around. At the same time, it was extremely comforting to be in my own place, in my own surroundings, and with my own things. And so, the recovery routine at home began.

Each day went by surprisingly quickly and was filled with self-care and rest - lots of rest. Mix in walking for exercise and making meals, and the days flew by. Once again, my wonderful neighbours were happy to help out and check in on me. I had some beautiful chats and visits with my two girls. It was great to see them, as well as have visits from friends and co-workers. It wasn't long before I was comfortable being up and about, although I was still tender. My energy wasn't 100 percent, so I still needed to rest a lot. But all in all, I felt great. So much so that I was able to travel.

Being alone for a few months, I missed socializing with others and was blessed one of my dear friends invited me to spend time with them at their place down south. Needless to say, I was so grateful and jumped at the chance! This was the first time I would fly with my proper passport. While it may not seem like a big deal, it was amazing how good it felt to finally be congruent. I was being seen for who I am, and not nervous about being outed by airport security or airline check-in staff. My official identification documents now matched my gender expression; everything matched. I was just another woman travelling to see her friends and that was so cool. This is an example of the huge stressor the transgender community experiences and that 99 percent of the population take for granted.[3] Yet, it is another burden we deal with.

[3]Sex and Gender Diversity Among Transgender Persons in Ontario, Canada: Results From a Respondent-Driven Sampling Survey Ayden I. Scheim & Greta R. Bauer Pages 1-14 | Published online: 21 Apr 2014

By this time, it was December in Canada and getting quite a bit cooler. I was cleared for travel by the doctors at the clinic, but not allowed in the water for a few more days after arriving at my friend's place. That was a small price to pay to be able to visit with my friends while completing my recovery. I am forever grateful and hopeful that I wasn't too much of a burden. I felt stronger and managed to be up and about spending a lot of time walking on the beach and in my friend's neighbourhood to build up my strength and stamina.

To say that we had a great time would be an understatement. As was typical when we got together, there was no lack of laughter and enjoying each other's company. Even just lounging quietly, getting some sun was somehow better while being with good friends. It was extremely therapeutic walking on the beach, and even better, receiving the email from the surgical staff clearing me to swim. I am a warm weather person and crave the heat. I'm positive that spending this short time near the water, my happy place, and being there with good friends, accelerated my recovery. I was sad when it all came to an end. But, I am very thankful I was able to do this.

Christmas came and went, and I was able to spend some time with my daughters, which is always a good thing. I tried to make the house as festive as I could with lots of colour and a bit of holiday spirit. I know it was hard for them, not being together as a family this time of year. It was probably another thing that changed within me. As I stated earlier, Christmas was never my thing. But, it suddenly became a fun time of year. I'm sure that confused the heck out of them, and I now realize, it's another thing I would have liked to be sensitive to. Sometimes, I wish there was a manual for all of this.

The New Year brought a time of renewal - a fresh start. I had been on my own for a few years now and had completed my transition, socially, legally, and finally, medically. I did a lot of personal work with my therapists to amplify my understanding of who I am. I wanted to get comfortable in my new skin, my correct skin, so I figured it was time to think about getting into a relationship, a romantic relationship. It was time to get back into the dating scene, which I found simply terrifying.

I have a network of professionals that include executive and life coaches. They are knowledgeable and talented people, and I am not ashamed to say I took advantage of their expertise. It was time for me to have a conversation with my good friend and coach. She wanted me to describe what I was looking for in a partner. So, I wrote down a few attributes. She read them and told me to be extremely detailed and try again. I went back to my list and wrote down a few more. Once again, she told me to be more detailed. This went back and forth for a few more iterations. Finally, I developed a list of about 25 attributes that entailed what I was really looking for in a partner. It was an invaluable exercise towards clarity, and I can't thank her enough for her patience and persistence.

> *She taught me that only when you*
> *know what you are truly looking for*
> *can you then begin your search.*

It's wasn't enough knowing what I didn't want, although that did help. But no, I also needed to be precise about what I wanted because I wasn't going to settle. After everything I went through, I knew that life is too short, and quite frankly, I'm too valuable not to find the best life has to offer me. I believe everyone needs to keep in mind that each of us is worthy and owe ourselves what we feel we deserve. I invested a lot of time getting to where I was, getting my act together, being happy as the person I truly am. I wasn't going to let anyone take that away from me. As a result, I was content with the fact I was either going to find the best possible match or be on my own a while longer. But, I wasn't going to rush into anything, that was for damn sure. I also expected this was going to be a long-term goal and would take quite a bit of time, so I figured the sooner I started, the better.

The dating scene in the LGBTQ+ community in a smaller city was challenging, to say the least. In particular, in the Lesbian community. Yes, I am gay, a woman attracted to women. It appeared that this initially caused a bit of confusion in my circle of friends and family. My story challenged the beliefs of many within society. There is a thought that physical sex assigned at birth matches gender and sets sexual orientation. In short, a person assigned male at birth, should be identified as a man for their gender and attracted to women. For many, this is a given. People now expected that when I transitioned to a woman that I would be attracted to men now. Nope, that's not how it works. They are not inextricably linked. Sex, gender, and sexual orientation are not predetermined by the other, and I am that case in point. Sex was assigned male at my birth, but my gender identity was as a woman. I was attracted to women prior to my transition, and I remain attracted to women. So, they are not linked, but rather, independent aspects of an individual. This is now who I am. A woman attracted to women.

January 15, 2018

When all you are trying to do is live your life as who you truly are, you aren't doing anything wrong.

But I digress, now back to dating. All this notwithstanding,

I was able to arrange to meet a handful of women for coffee dates. I met some really nice people. But, something didn't click with any of them because there was never a special connection. Apparently, this is quite a normal part of the process for everyone, and just because I am transgender, doesn't mean I don't have similar experiences in similar circumstances.

After a period of time, I got quite frustrated. I began to think I wasn't going to find anyone and would be alone for the rest of my life. Surprisingly, I wasn't that despondent. I had a good life, great friends, a good job, and lots of interests. But, I still wanted that special someone to experience my life with, to laugh with, share dreams and quiet times with, and to be friends and celebrate all that life has to offer. I was about to give up, and then it happened - she happened.

We met on an online site designed for people over 50 looking for a life-long relationship. I wanted to meet someone my age who understood the context of my life and times. I knew when I saw her picture, there was something there. That may sound shallow, but holy... the *click* was so incredibly audible. We first connected via text and email. We quickly started to chat via telephone calls. These discussions occurred every day, many times for over an hour. During these chats, we covered all the heavy topics, finances, religion, likes, dislikes, family, and what each of us was passionate about. The similarities were striking. Everything lined up, and it was amazing. I'm choosing not to share more detail about this initial stage of our relationship as it is a very private aspect of my and her life.

We quickly learned to appreciate our ability to discuss anything, work, family, friends, funny stories, literally anything. The fact we were on the same plane virtually all the time, made conversation and sharing natural and easy. Nothing was forced or awkward. It was great to have someone in my life who deeply listened and was supportive. The fact she was able to open up and be vulnerable and willing to let me into her life was equally amazing.

We finally met in person, and I knew she was the one. It was definitely love at first sight. Because we knew so much about each other before the meeting, I was already well down that road prior to our meeting. However, the last step was going to be the clincher for both of us. We both believe in the importance of physical connection, as well as every other level. I made it quite clear that I wanted her to be sure she felt that physical spark before we went any further. If there wasn't, I wanted her to let me know - no harm, no foul. I felt it was better to discover that early on, and I also didn't want her to feel she was settling. I didn't want to be the person she was settling for. I definitely wasn't going to settle, and I didn't want her to either. Suffice it to say that this was not an issue. We continued to see each other, and it became more apparent as time went on that this was turning into a serious and committed relationship.

This was just over two years ago at the time of me writing this. We are in a very committed permanent relationship. We are engaged and living in the same house we have created as our home. I am, rather, we are, ridiculously happy. I am so thankful for her love and support. Her parents and siblings are very welcoming, and we have a great time when we all gather together. I stated at the start of my journey that all I wanted was to live, love, and laugh for the rest of my life. I can happily say, *Mission accomplished!* Between us, we have three amazing daughters. Everyone gets along, and we are slowly connecting as a family as we settle into our new normal. It may take a while to get to a complete sense of being a blended family, but we enjoy time together, and we are all getting to know each other better.

So, I have accomplished my dream. All I am doing now is working at my job, contributing to the community, and living life as my authentic self. I feel this is something so many take for granted, and it is a struggle for those suffering with Gender Dysphoria. It has been a long and very lonely road at times, but I did it. I no longer have to worry about living a life of regret.

I have asked myself, Knowing what I know now,
would I do it all again?
And the answer is Absolutely.
Would I do things differently?
In many ways, yes, but in other ways, no.

I am often asked if I wish I would have done this earlier in my life. I reply that yes, of course I would have chosen to be my authentic self sooner and ended the pain and suffering earlier. However, I would not change my timeline because I wanted to be who my daughters needed as a father. I would not take away so many great memories of that time with them. Would I have handled certain aspects of my transition differently? Yes, absolutely ! I would have tried to minimize the impact on others better and be more attuned to their needs. Gender Dysphoria robbed me of the energy and ability to cope to a certain degree. If I could change anything, and I can't honestly say that I would have been able to, I would have wanted to be more aware and somehow find the energy to be a better person through it all.

As is the case for many things in my life, it is not what I did, but how I did it that leaves a mark. Each day and in every way, I am becoming a better person, and I try to demonstrate that in my life. It is easy to dismiss people perceived as different. But, their differences don't equate to them being wrong or bad;

it just means they are unique, and that is a wonderful thing. Trusting one's individuality is what makes the world, your world and my world, amazing. Treating everyone with dignity and respect is something many in the transgender community don't experience enough of. It doesn't cost anything, and sometimes, a welcoming smile is all that is needed. If someone reaches out, please take the call. Be that safe place. The little things make the most significant difference. Be that person.

Love yourself and always be humble and kind.

Epilogue

All things considered, I realize I am fortunate with how well my transition went. Most of that is due to planning and determination to see everything through to becoming my authentic self. As you can see, it wasn't easy, and there were many dark times. Unfortunately, I don't think the aspects that were easier for me are typical for others in similar circumstances. Many in the community suffer from the adverse effects of Gender Dysphoria. Many do not have access to the resources I did and need all the support they can get. My hope is that people understand that living with this is not a choice. Those making the decision to transition to be true to themselves, often have to make great sacrifices. Their family, friends, and work are all impacted. It is a monumental undertaking, and those moving through it deserve kindness, empathy, support and respect.

People often say I was very brave to transition. While I am thankful for their kind words, I remind them that I am not brave. It wasn't courage that motivated me to make this change; I did this out of necessity. To me, bravery is a decision to do something you don't have to do. You can either do something or not. Either way, your life will be relatively unaffected. I had no choice. If I wanted to survive, I had to transition - end of discussion. I see the people who supported me and who surround me still to this day as the brave ones. They made a choice to support me and were there when I needed them. I know they could have just as easily turned their backs on me with little impact on them. But instead, they made the active choice to stand with me, even if it meant facing ridicule within their social circles or having their belief system challenged by others. They are the brave ones. And to all of you, I send respect and a very heartfelt thank you for not compromising who you are.

While this was an extremely challenging time in my life, I managed to find a path through it all. There is no way around Gender Dysphoria; you have to work your way through it. In many ways, it was an invaluable experience in that I learned so much about myself and what I am capable of. I am not only content, happy and comfortable in my own skin, but much more resilient as a result of moving through this. It is amazing what you are capable of when something is necessary for your survival. I think people are more resilient than they think, although it can be difficult to access. There are times, at least for me, when I was strong, and other times, not so much. But deep down, I was finally able to grab hold of who I really was and accept that I wanted to survive. I became clear and determined that my goal was to survive. It's that determination that fed my ability to get through the tough times. Knowing that you are resilient and can be your true self, whatever that means to you, is an empowering thing.

So much of what I experienced can be true of any significant life event. Adversity is adversity, and I learned that it is okay to ask for help no matter what I am going through. No one is an expert in everything, and at some point, we all need support. That's okay. Ask. No one can help you if you don't let them know what you need. So many things in life can be overwhelming because there is no manual. Initially, I had no idea what to do, and then, I didn't know what to do first. I was overwhelmed not knowing how to tackle what I perceived to be an insurmountable task. That's when I finally asked for help and found a general therapist. Once that was initiated, I took the next step and sought a gender therapist. This piece was key to getting grounded in order for me to move forward in any shape or form.

Finding resources now is so much easier than it used to be. The internet is such a valuable source of information and can be a valuable tool. Its impact cannot be dismissed, and it is a great place to start, especially when looking for a support group and the community that resonates with you. For me, that was critical. From there, I was able to get a sense that I wasn't alone and that there were others in the same boat as me. This was a good place to start to try to find other available supports. Please don't try to re-invent the wheel. I was more than willing to use other's experiences to take advantage of the leg work they did to start creating a pathway. It is great to see more and more people not waiting and coming out when they are younger with more services and resources available for them than ever before. Again, start with the internet; its right there at your fingertips and such a great way to find support, interact with others in the community and track down sources for services you may require.

But that is not to say there is not more work to be done. While there are protections in place for transgender people in many jurisdictions, that is not the case everywhere. In Canada, we are fortunate to have laws protecting us, but that doesn't mean discrimination and hardships do not occur. They do. As such, I continually speak to groups of medical and legal professionals to bring awareness to the treatment of transgender people. I also offer educational and motivational keynote presentations to share my experience through my transition and inspire resilience to the general public, businesses, and organizations.

It is easy to feel the burden of being overwhelmed in life. I found the trick is not attempting to tackle everything at once. I initially didn't know where to start and tried doing too many things at once. Did that work? Nope. It was like trying to boil the entire ocean - not going to work. That is when I started understanding this was going to be a one day at a time journey. And that can be difficult to accept. I was in a hurry to get this all done. And who doesn't want to get through trauma as quickly as possible? I had to learn to let that go and be comfortable building the bridge as I crossed it. That can also be scary, no doubt. But it worked for me. And I didn't wait to finish the bridge before taking action.

To that end, the plan I created needed to be both safe and smart. The intention of implementing safety was to make sure I did everything in an environment that supported my mental, emotional and physical health. Hence the creation of my medical team. Because, as is the case with any major life change one faces, I needed to create a soft place to land. I knew there would be times I would veer off my path and end up in situations spinning my wheels, feeling like I was going backwards instead of moving forward. It was critical to have the support I required in place to catch me when I fell. And I fell a lot. It is so important that everyone finds a soft place to land in their life. I can't stress that enough.

That takes us to being smart. This meant creating a plan that was right for me. To acknowledge the needs of others around me that provided them with time to work through it and provide as much information as they wanted and needed in a manner that worked for them. Because everyone is different. Some need and can manage the pressure of the fire hose while others are much more comfortable with a slower drip from the faucet. Outside added stressors come with moving through any adversity, and it is important to be aware of this. One thing I recognized is that people around me, while being fully supportive, needed time to grieve. As I was celebrating my transition into the new me, they were mourning the old me they knew and loved. That was a huge error on my part, and a major lesson learned.

Now, all the pieces of the puzzle are in place. My future is bright, and I am excited about what life has in store for me moving forward. I have learned so much about myself and relationships. I like to think I will be better at both. I have worked very hard to get where I am today. I invested a lot of time and energy to become who I am, to be me. I want to be able to be in control and face life head-on from a position of strength. And here I am. I am no longer a stranger in the mirror. Each day I see my authentic self looking back at me, and that is an amazing feeling. Today, I am in a very committed relationship with a wonderful woman who I love deeply and who loves me. We have three amazing daughters between us, and we are working on becoming a family. My priorities are my family, and I try to bring my *A game* every day. Relationships are not 50-50. They are 100-100. I never want to bring only a 50 percent effort. That's a pretty low bar. 100 percent is the goal, every day. Because I am worth it as equally as they are.

In a relationship, 1+1=3. We are both individuals. I don't ever want to lose sight of that. I have invested so much in myself to evolve to who I am now. I don't ever what to lose myself, and I don't want that for my partner. In creating a relationship, just as we commit to ourselves, we commit to the connection we have created and nurtured. That is the third party in our relationship. Because it takes on a life and character of its own, it deserves that level of attention.

Finally, I hope that for those in the community, you are able to relate to some aspect of my story and, as a result, feel you are not alone and experience some degree of solace. For others, I hope you have gained insight as to what it means to suffer from Gender Dysphoria and that it is not a choice. Transitioning is a daunting undertaking and not for the faint of heart. We are all deserving of respect and dignity. Life is short, and your dead a long time. Live your life. Be the best you can be. Strive to bring out the best in others. Live, love, and laugh as your true authentic self. Be proud of who you are and live your life out loud.

Erin Leeann LeBlanc

I first met Erin across a boardroom table and was struck by her confident and insightful contribution to the meeting. Compelled to thank her and learn more I approached her afterwards. The ensuing exchange was brief yet established one fact – we connected. Emails sustained us until we could meet again over dinner. A classic chin wag with much laughter culminated in the best line of the night. I complimented her on her shoes and she blushingly confessed to being "such a girly, girl!". Then she told me her story.

Stranger in the Mirror is a detailed account of survival, resilience and finding peace and love. From extraordinary anguish through to "just another woman traveling to see her friends" Erin shares her thoughts, feelings, decisions and actions in a pressure filled, painful journey. She articulates her experience in a way that informs and inspires empathy for members of the trans community living their complicated existence. Careful not to prescribe her path as the only way, the details do, however, outline what a comprehensive and exhausting process it is to simply live as yourself.

Reading this book is like spending time with Erin. There's strength in her vulnerability and wit in her perspective. Woven throughout the pages are examples of what profound support looks like and her final words are a call to action. As a parent in the LGBTQ+ community I am sincerely grateful for that challenge to the world.

Karyn Garossino – Olympian, M.Ed.,
Owner, Horizon Coaching, Corporate Trainer,
Third Factor Inc., Toronto, Ontario, Canada

About the Author
Erin Leeann LeBlanc, MEd, LLM

Photo by Suzy Lamont

Ms. LeBlanc is a Director within Smith School of Business and a member of the faculty as an adjunct lecturer teaching International Trade Law in graduate programs offered by the School. In 2017, she was the recipient of the *Tri-Award (accessibility, equity, & human rights)* from Queen's University for her work in establishing transgender transitioning guidelines and identifying and removing barriers for individuals transitioning in the workplace.

As an advocate for the LGBT community focusing on assisting transgender people, Erin is quoted in print and online media. She is a co-host of a weekly radio show speaking to current issues and stories that impact the transgender community. She is also actively involved in conducting seminars for organizations in both the public and private sectors regarding access to legal and medical services for people in the transgender community. She is also a frequent motivational speaker at events and continues to do both keynote speeches and training meetings for all sizes and types of organizations.

A graduate of Queen's University in Economics and Psychology, she also holds a Master's Degree in Higher

Education Policy from the University of Toronto, as well as being a graduate of Queen's Master of Law Program specializing in International Trade Law.

She is the parent of two daughters and currently resides in Ottawa, Ontario, Canada with her partner and their dog.

CPSIA information can be obtained
at www.ICGtesting.com
Printed in the USA
LVHW022025160820
663340LV00024B/692